THE EYE
THAT SEES
ITSELF

Shimon Malin

MORNING LIGHT PRESS

First Edition
Published by Morning Light Press, 2004.

Morning Light Press
323 North First, Suite 203
Sandpoint, ID 83864
www.morninglightpress.com
info@mlpress.com

Printed on acid-free paper in Canada.

ISBN: 1-59675-002-2

Malin, Shimon, 1937-
  The eye that sees itself : beyond the subject/object mode : experiences
and reflections / by Shimon Malin.-- 1st ed.
     p. cm.
  Includes bibliographical references and index.
  ISBN 1-59675-002-2 (alk. paper)
  1. Awareness. 2. Self-realization.
  3. Metaphysics. 4. Knowledge, Theory of. 5. Mysticism. I. Title.
  BF1999.M2355 2004
  128--dc22

                         2004017320

This

book

is dedicated

to the memory of

Amnon Ben-Zvi,

a fellow seeker

and a

true friend.

Into the house she came and bowed her head.
And it was spring. "Come out," her servant prayed,
"Rabi'a, come out and see what God has made."
"Come in and see the maker." Rabi'a said.

Author's Preface

This collection of essays traces its origin to the influence of two spiritual masters, William Segal and Franklin Merrell-Wolff.

I had the good fortune to be associated with William Segal for thirty-five years, from 1965 until his death in 2000. Whatever understanding I have acquired in spiritual matters is due to his teaching.

By contrast, I have never met Franklin Merrell-Wolff. Nevertheless, I was deeply impressed by his writings about "consciousness without an object," and the possibility of "introception." Introception, according to Merrell-Wolff "is to be understood as the process whereby consciousness turns upon itself and moves towards its source."[1] The present essays are largely about the process of transcending the subject/object mode of perception and moving towards introception. I even contemplated naming the book, *Towards Introception*, an idea I dropped when I realized that the word "introception" is unknown to most people, and, furthermore, it may be confused with the word "introspection," which means something different altogether.

The essays contained in this volume were written over many years, from the early 1980s to 2000.

I would like to point out, that throughout the book I use the term *objective* as "pertaining to an object" rather than "having actual existence," which is the more common usage. Likewise, *subjective* is being used as "pertaining to a subject" rather than "existing only in an individual's mind."

Having greatly benefited from the study and practice of the teaching of G. I. Gurdjieff, I could not avoid using, on occasion, some of his terminology, and, in particular, the terms "self-remembering" and "identification." I believe that it is possible to get the gist of most essays without familiarity with these and other Gurdjieffian terms. However, the two terms mentioned above do convey precise meaning that need practice in order to be understood. The best available introduction to their meaning is contained in P. D. Ouspensky's book[2], *In Search of the Miraculous*.

1. F. Merrell-Wolff, *Transformations in Consciousness*, SUNY Press, Albany, New York, 1995, p. 104.

2. P. D. Ouspensky, *In Search of the Miraculous*, Harcourt, Brace & World, New York, 1949, pp. 117–122, 150–151.

CONTENTS

Opening the book,

Turning a page,

"Ahh!"

Body,

Infused with subtlety,

Melts away.

Empty pages are full,

Filled pages—empty.

Only seer is.

Shall we look at another page?

STILLNESS AND SEEING

Stillness is not a state, it is an inner place. Like a hub at the center of a wheel, it accommodates with equal ease quietude and movement. In itself it has nothing to do with either quietude or movement. How does it participate in the phenomenal world?

—What is Self-Remembering?, page 9

Part I

The Inner Dimension

As I sat in meditation this morning I saw clearly the need to attend to the inner, the unobjectivized. Whenever the attention was directed there, and was freed from the habitual mode of looking at an inner screen on which objects appeared, I felt energized and nourished.

The inner dimension is where life is. Consequently, thoughts that are not coming from that wellspring, are mere mechanical productions.

In fact, much of the spiritual instruction we receive is a way of suggesting this 180-degree turn of the attention. Take, for example, the instruction "Be still!" In the ordinary mode of outward orientation one cannot be still. On the other hand, "Be still and know that I am" clearly shows that the attention needs to be inwardly oriented. "I am" will not be found by gazing at objects on an inner screen!

Oriented inwardly, I feel a dynamic stillness, one that is not contradictory to a feeling of a deep movement. As I continue to look, I see the interface between the personal and the impersonal—and then the transition to the impersonal takes place. The sensing of this transition has to do with a change in the level of meaning: the usual, personal kind disappears and is replaced by a meaning without content or context. Going even deeper one discovers a layer that does not carry meaning because it is the source of meaning. The experience of meaning is a dualistic one; this deeper layer is not dualistic.

How is the attention to be directed to the inner dimension? The attempts to somehow forcibly shut off the outer don't work. It is a question of being interested in the inner to such an extent that the outer naturally subsides. This interest can arise from a compelling interest in the deeper impressions, as they enter. Actually, at the center of every impression is the opportunity to transcend the inner/outer duality! To reach this center, the pleasure that is there when the feelings are alive to the impressions must be surrendered; or at least the identification with this pleasure, the orientation toward it must be surrendered. This act of surrender is the interface or the bridge between the personal and the impersonal.

Stopping. Seeing.

An overcast day in late fall. I sit at a long table, with others. There is a flow of conversation, accompanied by outer gestures, animated by inner experiences. Come to think of it, it is a complex interplay of energies— mine, the others', the room and its furniture, the ideas we are discussing. I am involved, absorbed, steeped in it.

Even though my attention is occupied, my glance wanders. And then— suddenly—my eyes stop, and my attention joins them: a plain red building with grey roof and brick chimney is visible through the window. I have seen it many times, but now I really see it. Surrounded and partly concealed by bare branches and bare trunks, it is a beautiful sight. This view, framed by the window—home, trees, fence, road, grey sky—expresses perfectly the place, the day and the season: New England at the end of fall, awaiting the onslaught of winter.

As I continue to look and enjoy, the seer is included. My attention is directed inward now as well as outward, and I acknowledge the mellowness of the feelings, the prerequisite to the experience of beauty.

This moment is a subtle crossroads. Will I merely enjoy, or will the attention delve for its source? I stop. The seeing deepens. I stop again. Who sees? Who asks the question? The experience is like diving into a sea, where the essential happening is out of sight, with only fragments accessible for description. Flashes of understanding bring a conclusion in their wake: Whenever I see "some thing," the seeing is limited; what I see as "some thing" is always a mental construct. And any "thing" I see can become transparent under the continued gaze of attention.

I stop again, and see that I've lost it. The attention, narrowed down through the fascination of forming a conclusion, no longer brings me the food of impressions, the blessings of beauty. And yet, at this very moment, as I stop and see myself, I can affirm a presence that can become whole, and wholly Me—as soon as I let go.

The afternoon progresses, the rain has stopped. I look out the window. A car passes by. An expansive laziness sets in. My glance descends into the vague reflection of the window on the polished table. I am aware, right now, of an aching heart—a response to the realization of how much I am missing in my ordinary life, moment by moment, day in and day out.

On Seeing and Understanding

As I sit in front of the computer with the intention of writing, I begin by looking at myself and am immediately impressed by this realization: It is wonderful that no matter what state I am in, the act of looking begins an ascent. It is as if the very nature of consciousness is to move one upward toward freedom. All I need to do is keep out of the way.

Clearly, for the process to continue, I must continue to be there—present, looking, seeing. And I see that the call to do so is not without its pitfalls. An act of seeing triggers a mental activity, that of formulating or of "knowing" what I have seen. This leads, in turn, to fixating on the formulation. When this happens, I am no longer seeing myself. I am now looking at a mental construct. My attention is no longer free. The ascent is arrested.

Just as I was impressed a few minutes ago by the power of seeing, I am impressed at this moment by the power of understanding. The intention not to become identified with mental constructs leads to a clear perception of the distinction between seeing and formulating and to the arising of the intention to stay with the seeing. When I am able to see without giving in to an inclination to formulate, my field of awareness naturally expands.

So, in the span of a few minutes I have witnessed the ease of opening and the obstacle to opening. We are subject to both grace and gravity.

This realization gives one pause. Does nature favor our conscious evolution or is our work "going against nature?" This seems to depend on what we mean by the word *nature*. If we mean the whole of the ray of creation, then nature leaves the gates wide open to the possibility of our conscious evolution. There is however, a more restricted usage of the word *nature*—the alive, yet unselfconscious aspect of things. This nature knows nothing of conscious evolution, and our (unavoidable) participation in it keeps us imprisoned in a web of identifications.

From this perspective, the importance of seeing and understanding becomes clear. Understanding can guide our intention toward opening to consciousness. And seeing is the concrete activity that, in its quiet and innocuous way, challenges the tremendous power that the unconscious aspect of nature wields over us.

What Is Self-Remembering?

I am sitting here watching the slow movements of clouds. And as I do, I connect with the possibility of watching myself as well—looking beyond the tensions and into a layer that, when objectivized, is empty.

I discover that stillness is not a state; it is an inner place. Like a hub at the center of a wheel, it accommodates quietude and movement with equal ease. In itself it has nothing to do with either quietude or movement. How does it participate in the phenomenal world? This is a mystery.

Stillness is the place where the phenomenal and noumenal worlds interface. It is the opening through which subtle vibrations can reach us, and so reach the phenomenal world. Remembering oneself is the act of creating and maintaining this opening.

Putting the idea of self-remembering at the center of one's practice is the genius of the Gurdjieff work. Self-remembering is the foundation. The question, "Can I keep remembering myself as I get up and take a few steps?" is as simple as it is profound. A few moments of relatively pure engagement with this effort—an engagement without reaction, where realization of forgetting becomes remembering—and the world becomes beautiful.

Such a relatively pure effort brings a spaciousness that can accommodate whatever state the body–mind is in. And when we are able to see ourselves, that body–mind state no longer claims center stage. The dichotomy of *wish for change* versus *resistance to change* loses its power—so change can actually take place.

The Importance of Seeing

One can never overestimate the importance of seeing. This was reinforced this afternoon as again and again I came back to self-observation. In the beginning I repeatedly saw in myself a state of being dispersed. However, as things slowly quieted down, the way from dispersion and identification to presence and openness became very clear.

At first there was simply recognition of the difference between a state without awareness and the same state *with* awareness. And of course, when awareness was present, the state itself began to change.

I then saw that when awareness was present, I could be aware of many things, but the important thing was to be aware of the attention. As I followed my attention and saw its dispersion, its unrootedness, its attachment to objects, a shift took place. The attention moved into a place that is deeper than mind; it moved to include the subject, myself.

Since the attention was no longer glued to the projections of mind, there was something in that state that felt and was ineffable. This something could be communicated indirectly, and only to those who had had the experience themselves. The inclusion of both subject and objects in the field of the attention is a transcendence of the subject/object mode. Being between Subject and object is akin to being in the middle ground, between Self and self.

We often speak of the need for the mind, body and feelings to be related, and there is no denying the importance of that. The experiences of the afternoon, however, showed that it is even more important for the attention to be unified. And the attention can only be unified by occupying the middle ground. Isn't this what self-remembering really is? When self remembers Self, an attention connects them. I am here, present to both. This is the condition of potential openness to a higher vibration.

Stillness and Time

Now, as I get in touch with the feel of Self, I am relatively released from the sense of time. I see a relationship between being dominated by self (with lowercase "s") and being obsessed with the feeling of the passage of time. Krishnamurti says, "Time is thought," and he is right. Intermittently, I see a stillness that includes a cessation of the sense of time. This sense of time has very little to do with ascertaining the time by looking at a clock. A moment ago I was relatively still; this stillness was not interrupted in the least when I looked at a clock and found out what time it was.

Plato wrote, "Time is the moving image of eternity." There is a sense in which time and eternity are related. First, both are related to the Subject, and neither is objectivizable. That is to say in the world of objects, both inner and outer, we find neither eternity nor time. Second, as I follow the transition from a moment of stillness to a resumption of inner movement, I see the sense of time arise as a kind of involution of the experience of stillness: it is as if the crispness of stillness degenerates to become the sense of time.

Now I become aware of a relationship between seeing and stillness. Seeing itself, as opposed to naming (not to mention thoughts and feelings that arise), takes place in stillness; it is not associated with time. In this sense, the phrase "timeless seeing" is a redundancy.

The Power of Seeing

A bright, sunny morning. I had to draw the curtain over the window to prevent glare. No sun in my heart, though. I am slightly depressed by the advance of the Parkinson's, and possibly as a side effect of the medication for its symptoms.

So as I sit down to write, I feel as if I were walking in a desert, plugging along without much hope, with only an underlying despair (Emerson's "quiet desperation") for company. In this moment it occurs to me that what I am experiencing now is awaiting everybody in old age; and also that it is less severe than an unexpected diagnosis of impending death. What I am facing is the decay of the body. A slow decay, in my case, and with luck, even reversible in a few years if breakthroughs occur. But I can't count on that. So this morning, I face decay and uncertainty.

As I look, I realize the power of seeing. The underlying slight depression may be chemically induced, as I mentioned. This can't be changed, and it belongs to the phenomenal level. The seer, however, is quite unaffected. To the extent that instead of identification with thoughts and feelings I can become the seer, I am free of my state.

As I do that, I discover, unexpectedly, a tinge of joy. Unexpected, because my notion of the seer is one of total neutrality, an emptiness like that of a mirror. The joy comes from somewhere else; there is joy in me as I identify with the seer. In other words, there is joy in seeing!

Seeing is always the same and always fresh. Moreover, it derives its capacity to nourish from its seeing nature, not from the content that is seen. Because it is always the same and still always fresh, the seeing belongs to the noumenal world. And yet, since what is seen are phenomena, it is related to the phenomenal world as well. In fact, seeing is the interface between the phenomenal and the noumenal.

Furthermore, seeing is one kind of doing—doing without interference. But there is another kind of doing that comes from the noumenal, a kind of doing that is based on the sword of discrimination. It is interference from a higher level—interference in the happenings on the phenomenal level. And yet, it is non-doing as far as the ego is concerned. I see the production of joy as a small example of that. This example reveals the nature of this second kind of doing as emanation from a higher level—very different from ordinary doing.

MIND

What happens when I stay with the thought "I"? First, the attention

encompasses the body. Then there is an expansion in physical space

(beyond the body), and also a kind of expansion that makes physical

space feel flat, as if it were just a surface. This other kind of expansion is,

I suppose, related to a movement into the unobjectivized.

—*The Place of Mind, page 33*

An Exploration of Dissatisfaction

I wish to explore the state of dissatisfaction I am in at this moment.

This state of dissatisfaction comes hand-in-hand with thoughts about what I could do to assuage it, none of which is really attractive. I'll stay with the state itself.

Now I realize that a part of the state is the wish to resolve, change it. The implication is that it's not OK to be in this state. Well, suppose I stay in it forever, try to make my home there.

Something changes, just a bit. I look at myself, being dissatisfied. I am still dissatisfied, but some unpleasant edge is no longer there. In addition to the dissatisfied one, someone else is present, watching.

Still staying just as I am, neither anticipating nor trying to bring about change, I am no longer victimized by the state. I feel an impersonal richness underneath it. For example, it seems that the impressions coming in from the outside world are feeding something in me.

This is not an easy out. The dissatisfaction is still present. But now it is not the only item in the field of my attention. More is present. Yet, there is a quality about this state of dissatisfaction that says, "It is not acceptable to stay like this."

Now something changes in the body, an opening at the bottom of the spine, and an energy flow. This opening is related to the impersonal self and to a unitive state. Following it, I go in and out of a state of no differentiation.

Even though a weakened version of the dissatisfaction is still present, I see it now as grist for my mill.

I am interested, at this moment, in the impersonal side, which I can be momentarily at will. Inwardly, there is just a space; outwardly, there is perception, without reaction—clean perception. In the body there is energy flow, related to the spine, which is not "mine."

The pull away from the present comes from the dissatisfied aspect, which wishes for change. The impersonal has no inclination toward anything that is not what it is now.

Here are some deductions that follow from the experience: First, the way out of suffering is through the impersonal self. Second, the impersonal is always there, but the attention is not always with it. From this follows, third, that the key is the placement of the attention.

All of this is subtle. The idea is not to run away from the personal side, not to use the impersonal to avoid personal suffering. Rather, the idea is to *include* the personal in the impersonal, and thus avoid being victimized by the suffering. The victimization occurs because, in a state that is purely personal, the suffering is overlaid with identification that implies it is not merely of the moment, but that this suffering is the total reality, that there is nothing else present and nothing else possible. By contrast, the presence of both the personal and impersonal sides allows the suffering to be present simply as an aspect of the moment, and not more—which is its true place.

So I return to looking at the dissatisfaction that is still present. As the looking intensifies, the personal dissolves, and seems to become merely a set of subtle emotional tensions with no "I" attached to them. It is now clear that the "I" in "I am dissatisfied" is an addition to the fact, an imputation by thinking. This leads to an amazing conclusion: In reality, there is no personal aspect! It appears when the mind, functioning in the dark, adds it to the actual event. When the light of clear attention shines on the happening, this imputation dissolves!

This opens up a much bigger question. Is there an actual state of affairs that can be known by pure seeing? Or is it true that there is nothing that is *just there*, waiting to be seen? Is it true that everything I see, even when my seeing is as untainted as it can be, is a *product of the seeing?*

As I look at this question, these conclusions surface: True seeing is unitive, a merging of the seeing and the seen. In such unitive seeing there is no content. The transition from this unitive seeing to seeing something is a bifurcation or splitting of the One; so, what is seen depends on the rift, so to speak. This last idea is speculation. And the question of the relation between seeing and reality is a deep one.

On Knowledge

The common use of the word *knowledge* has not only obscured understanding, but actually contributed to the confusion between real knowledge and informational knowledge.

Real knowledge is a merging of high vibrations with the totality of the body–mind complex. It can be contrasted with informational knowledge, which is merely a deposition of data in memory.

It follows that the acquisition of real knowledge entails a change in the person. One's faculties and capacities change; one's perception is different. And one can do what was impossible to do before.

The confusion between real knowledge and informational knowledge (and the common use of the word *knowledge* in the latter sense) has obscured the understanding that the acquisition of real knowledge is a sacred process. The ancients understood this well. For Plato, acquiring knowledge meant being in communion with the world of Forms. In the Old Testament, the verb "to know" is used in the sense of intimacy and merging. The acquisition of knowledge is not only a process of transformation for the one who comes to know; it is also a process of creation for the world at large.

Perhaps it is the relationship between knowledge and unknowing that is confusing to ordinary mind. The acquisition of real knowledge presumes that one is aware of one's unknowing (otherwise one tries to fill a full cup).

Once acquired, a truly profound knowledge becomes a part of one's being, and is fully compatible with the openness of unknowing.

The Personal Element

The impetus that brings me to the journal to write is the feeling that this activity is somehow meaningful. When I imagine other activities, they feel relatively unimportant. This presumed significance of writing has two aspects—the hope of discovering something of value that will help toward, let's say, enlightenment (not directly, necessarily; but perhaps it will lead to a better understanding of the obstacles); and secondly, there is the beneficent effect of the activity itself. Ordinarily writing in this way brings me to a more balanced and more awake state.

With this impetus comes the feeling that as I am engaged in this activity I am in control of the process of (let's call it) my development, because I am following it closely. In fact, this feels like an obstacle, the obstacle of the head wanting to stay in control.

What actually happens is partly a head-directed activity, and partly a spontaneous flow—in spite of the head's keeping a close watch. So, I don't feel that this obstacle disqualifies the activity. I do feel that it needs to be taken into account, and I am not sure how to do that.

Because the body is not really separate from thoughts, I experience this feeling of the head's maintaining control as a sensation in the stomach. This sensation is associated with fear, a fear that is the result of being ungrounded in myself. (Being "grounded" in the head is not being grounded in myself!)

Now I recognize this sensation and this fear as being recurrent—I know it well. And the connection I've made between it and the head usurping the place of my totality is an important discovery. *As long as I am in the head, I am ungrounded and afraid.*

A connection to my childhood arises at this point. I recall taking refuge in the head during a difficult period at ages nine and ten. I felt a certain layer of ego being formed there. This inner place became a strange sort of sanctuary—a bad place, but familiar and mine—free of surprises, free of uncertainties. The alternative is the openness of life, where there is no guarantee, lots of uncertainty, and potential novelty at any moment.

Why am I afraid and ungrounded when I am in the head? Because I am out of touch with what's going on. The emotions and the body are the instruments for being in touch. Ultimately, the feeling of safety that accompanies being in this bad place is an illusion. I can avoid being aware of what's going on by attending exclusively to thought, but what's going on will catch up with me. This brings a generalized state of anxiety—I don't know when or how it will catch up with me, or how bad it will be. There is a vague anticipation that it will be very bad—because as long as it is not, I will be able to continue with this mechanism of escape, that is staying absorbed in the world of thought.

Transparency

At this moment I see two possibilities: attending to a mental construct or attending to no-thing.

Relaxation and joy are spreading through the body. Whatever appears to the attention appears with a kind of transparency. There is no contradiction between content and nothingness. Both are present.

As I relax, a flow enters me. In my ordinary mode, tension blocks this entry. But now I am just sitting here, wishing for nothing, not even to know what is taking place.

Freedom from the known. No attraction to it. I follow sensations, and discover that there is mystery at their center. I am nourished by the mystery.

In one sense it is a mystery, in another it is something that is in plain view. It is mysterious to the mind, but in itself it just is.

At this moment I feel myself as "an entity that is no-entity." As such I see that simple attention to the moment is the way out of the tyranny of mentation. When the attention is truly on the moment, it is free of the clamor of thought, because thought, by its very nature, attends to products of the past.

The movement toward opening starts, then, with relaxation. This allows the attention to be unfocused and undirected, but very much here, moving toward identity with the whole field of awareness. This condition reveals that the structure of attention is complex. For example, the integration of awareness and attention does not prevent a small part of my attention from remaining with "things," allowing me to go on typing. Evidently, there is more than one quality or level of attention, and these different levels can do their jobs simultaneously and harmoniously.

The Structure of Sacrifice

Seeing and acceptance are the preconditions for the sacrifice of thoughts, emotions, desires and power needs.

When the higher appears in one, these lower elements lose their attraction. But for the higher to appear, they must first be sacrificed *while* they are attractive. It is a question of energetics: the energy that is released by the act of sacrifice is the energy that is transformed, the energy that by this very act gains an ability to connect to the higher.

Sacrifice is the opposite of repression. Repression is holding on to attachments. When they are relegated to the unconscious, they are fixated in the psyche, without possibility of release. Sacrifice is a genuine release.

The Place of Mind

What happens when I stay with the thought "I"? First, the attention encompasses the body. Then there is an expansion in physical space (beyond the body), and also a kind of expansion that makes physical space feel flat, as if it were just a surface. This other kind of expansion is, I suppose, related to a movement into the unobjectivized.

The seeing continues. A movement to full acceptance of what is seen brings energy to the spine, a feeling of presence and a change in the sense of self. This is magical. There is someone present now that was not present before. The new energy, or presence, has no words. *This shows that I need to move away from mind.*

At this moment the attention and the mind are directed toward this presence. This means that I am separate from it. Can this separation be overcome by an intentional movement? Having raised the question, I become aware of the arising of feeling. The feeling is related to the understanding that *the mind will never get it*. Always, it will be a question of moving away from mentation, struggling, perhaps, with chaos and confusion, managing, or not managing to come to the point of no separation. The arising of feeling in this context is a signal that I am reaching a significant truth.

Even so, the mind has a part to play. It can serve as a reminder, nudging us to begin the inner movement. But, just like a relative who sends us off on a journey, it must remain on the platform, waving, wishing us *bon voyage*. Later it can even help by sending us messages, the results of its understanding. Such messages, appearing at the right moment, can help us steer in the right direction. But the journey begins by moving away from identification with thought. For this voyage is controlled by something else altogether.

Why must the mind be left behind? One reason has to do with the level of vibrations. Mental operations are too slow. A different (and complementary) way of looking at it is this: Identification with thought makes it impossible for a third force to appear.

Consider an example. Suppose I wish for a change in myself. Instantly, there is a clash of forces in me, with the wish to change battling inertia. The third force is a full acceptance of how I am now, a nonmental agreement that change is not required. This acceptance cannot appear as long as my attention is identified with the thought, "I wish to change." Thought is not subtle enough to harbor paradoxes, and this quest contains paradoxes at every turn. For example, the realization that there is nothing to attain is crucial for transformation (or attainment) to take place.

If mentation is to be left behind, why even engage in these thoughts? I believe that a clear mental understanding of the place of mind is conducive to convincing mind to take its proper place.

Empty Cognizance

The wish to experience the nature of experiencing is my way in. Looking at myself now, I see a certain level of inner connection already established by remembering the question. And with this inner connection, comes a capacity to see more precisely the workings of the inner world.

The key to progress in this exploration is to look for a different kind of attention. The search changes from "What do I see now?" to "How do I see now?"

This exploration is closely related to the question, "Who am I?"—a question I find problematic. Often I take it as "What is my sense of 'I' now?" which, in fact, neatly avoids the issue, because it does not relate to the *potential* experiences of "I."

However, connecting this question, "Who am I?" to the question, "What is the attention with which I function now?" gives it depth. Regarding the attention, I am concerned with its potential to be unitary; this spills over to the question of identity.

My avoidance of the question, "Who am I?" seems related to the fact that the word "I" is automatically interpreted as a personal self. This interpretation preempts the possibility of exploring the impersonal domain, the domain of real Self. Seeing this limitation may help transcend it; at any rate, this limitation does not pertain to the exploration of the attention.

I have been impressed by Tulku Urgyen's reference to the nature of mind as "empty cognizance." In addition to attention and self, the nature of cognizance is another intriguing question. Primarily, what is consciousness, or the moment of cognizance, in itself, and secondarily, what is its relation with the gray stuff between my ears? As I was about to write these questions down, I had a moment of seeing that cognizance is different—perhaps even unrelated to—this body, so that the primary question felt much more urgent than the secondary one.

At first glance, the following distinction seems important: awareness without cognition (being aware without realizing that I am aware) in contrast to awareness *with* cognition (seeing while being aware that I see). There is however, a third category—the experience of flashing back and knowing in hindsight that I was aware of myself seeing. This brings me to a new realization: The question of my state in time (past, present and future) is not so important. Because when I establish the inner connection, I establish it for all times. (Like any new insight, this expression of it is lame, even deficient. It will improve in time.) This may be the esoteric meaning of atoning for past sins.

This new insight, however ineptly expressed, gave me a jolt into a new level. At once, I see the inner Work as more alive and less dualistic (this is an interesting duality!). This new level is sustained by a feeling of wholeness, based on a sensation in the hara. At this new level, I clearly see the intellect as a distinction-creating apparatus, doing its thing against the background of a holistic presence. When the mind is unaware of this background, the entities it creates seem to be separate and unrelated. Yet when the mind is aware of the background, these distinctions are not in contradiction to the fundamental fact of wholeness.

Another flash of insight: The event of enlightenment redeems not only the future (because one stays enlightened) but also the past. In truth, one's lack of enlightenment in the past is actually a *part* of the enlightened state of affairs, an aspect of one's timeless enlightenment. This insight leads to an expansion away from duality. I remember Gurdjieff's condemnation of the duality of good and evil: It brings one into such a narrow space! And when "good" is associated with enlightenment, the predicament becomes a knot (in R.D. Laing's sense of the term), a predicament that makes one more and more hopelessly imprisoned, as one attempts to come to unity by siding with one pole of a duality!

No Mind

Clearly, this deeper awareness is not *my* awareness—there is nothing

personal about it. It is *an awareness*, coming from, going to, connected

with an infinite space.

                              —*Experiencing, page 46*

The Sound of No-Sound

I

"Refuse any means of escape."

Here I am, on the cusp—looking, or attempting to look inward, into the subject. As I try, an outwardly oriented activity ceases. For an instant, everything becomes inner. The attempt to look inward, which started out as a sharply focused one, becomes relaxed, widely focused. Small self, with whom I am still identified, affirms the spacious presence of a Seeing, seeing through a non-doing presence.

If the one who is asking "Who am I?" is left out of the question, the query becomes meaningless. To be sure, the question may expand until the questioner dissolves, but until he or she does, the one who asks is the center of the question, the "I" of the moment. Now, keeping this in mind, I look inward—and this "I" does dissolve, offering a glimpse of another "I," one that appears related to a vast background space.

It becomes obvious that this is a hopeless quest for the inquiring mind. Because the mind is not "I" at all—it is more like a contraction that I am identified with. And the question cannot be answered as long as this inquiring mind, thus identified, is there.

As long as the inquiring mind is present, the direct way into the experience of Self involves going through this experience of the inquiring mind looking for itself—and finding nothing. This nothing is its demise.

This demise is an opening to a more awakened state. While the inquiring mind was present, it took center stage. Now that it is absent, it is not missed. Not at all.

II

The approach to Self is through spaciousness. This spaciousness is more than an expansive feeling. It is a deep relaxation in the background as well as the foreground of oneself.

Such a relaxation implies the dissolution of meaning-structures. This leads to the freedom to adopt new meaning-structures, even to adopt, at different times, meaning-structures that contradict each other. This flexibility leads to empathy—an appreciative sharing of another's meaning-structure.

An obstacle to such an opening is desire, the directing of the attention toward something to be attained in the future. Obviously, this takes the attention away from the true experience of now.

It is good for the attention to be spacious, yet this spaciousness is not the goal. One has a persistent feeling of a "mysterious something else," which can be experienced but not described, for which spaciousness is the gateway.

III

Where am I? Who am I? The sound of the brook enters through the open window. Who am I? How do I prepare for the experience that answers this question?

The mind waits. The space of waiting becomes filled with sounds— hammering in the distance, the ticking of a clock, the brook. Who listens? As

I become quieter, the space of listening opens up. There is enough space now for all the different sounds to be received, graciously and simultaneously, like welcomed guests. The listener has dissolved.

Can I listen *to the space that receives these sounds*? An underlying space appears, a space without space, supporting the space that receives the sounds. This supporting background is closer to "I," though not yet "I." The words "background" and "closer to I" indicate that as the mind tries to see this supporting space, there is a point beyond which it cannot go—the space disappears into its background, accompanied by a feeling that one is making contact with a deeper level.

Every sound received enters and becomes no-sound, but does not dissolve. The more open I am, the deeper this no-sound travels—and the more fully its own inner octaves resonate.

As I am engaged in this listening, fatigue disappears, malaise vanishes. There is intense interest. It is unlike ordinary interest, which is interest in something. This interest is both deeper (engaging deeper parts of myself) and content-free. It follows the seeing itself.

Now, there is an intimation of the unity of sound and listener that appears when the mind steps aside. No-mind receiving no-sound. From this vantage point it is clear that ordinary sounds are *produced* by the mind, out of incoming impressions, the innate nature of which is more akin to no-sound than to sound.

From the present perspective the source of the recurrent underlying feeling of dissatisfaction that plagues me and others reveals itself as the hunger to be in touch with deeper parts of oneself, to receive impressions deeply.

Experiencing

The richness of the world of feelings is present at every moment, at this moment. Yet the one who experiences it is not the ordinary self. The ordinary self is head-based, and the head is too slow, too coarse. The idea of emptiness is designed to lead me away from this self, to empty myself of it. This emptying cannot be done by the ordinary self. It cannot be deliberate. Rather, it must spring from the question, "Who am I?"

The inroads I've made into this question reveal that the ordinary sense of self is actually a mental construct. It is associated with tensions, which can be released. I looked into the eyes of an infant and, at that instant, neither of us was an ordinary self.

So—how about this moment? It is essential not to try anything. When I am not trying anything, feelings naturally arise. I experience the distinction between myself as an entity associated with the body and the rest of the world as strange. Relaxation spreads through the body. I am in touch with my yin side—undifferentiated, not concerned with time, subtly joyous to just be here. I look at myself, and am very clear about the difference between looking and the subsequent formulation of what I see. There is the looking, and then the head gets into action and formulates.

Right now, I am aware of the uniqueness of this moment, of this experience. Any wish for it to be different is an obstruction of the natural flow.

The feeling of emptiness—I am present, yet no one is present. The mind moves, and I witness this movement from a place that is no-place. I feel some longing, and can see at once the choice between being identified with this longing or separate from it.

My ordinary sense of self comes from the patterns that connect my attention to thinking. When these patterns change, my sense of self changes too.

The experience of emptiness comes on different levels. It begins when a subject sees nothing in the space where he looks. Then there is another level, a merging into a different state, where it is impossible to see "something." This state takes me from my ordinary self to another place altogether. For example, I may enter it from a mental state, and emerge feeling my body relax. I reach this state by being open to ordinary experiences as they come, being interested in experiencing their depths.

At this moment I feel my limitation as a level of subtle tension that does not go away. However, underneath it there is an awareness without limitations. This is a paradox: The degree of openness is limited by the tensions, and yet, in another sense, it is not limited at all. Clearly, this deeper awareness is not *my* awareness—there is nothing personal about it. It is *an awareness*, coming from, going to, connected with an infinite space.

Inner Presence

The inner presence is unconditional. It is here, unchanging and inviolate, independent of body and mind. What is its relationship with these phenomenal aspects of oneself?

For the most part I am simply unaware of the inner presence. Unconsciously, this lack of awareness generates the feeling of being in exile. Moment by moment, something essential is missing. Vaguely, I am aware of this lack, but the clear experience of inner presence makes the nature of what is missing known to me. With it, I lack nothing. Without it, I can be free of the feeling of lack only temporarily and intermittently.

This state of affairs must mean that being connected to the inner presence has a cosmological function. My need for it must be a reflection of an objective need.

The current Western worldview is based on the tacit or explicit assumption that the material universe is self-subsisting. Yet, one's need for contact with the inner presence indicates that, far from being self-subsisting, the material world is the product of the outwardly directed thrust of consciousness. The disharmony in the Western way of life is due to the comparative weakness of the inwardly directed thrust of consciousness.

Perhaps our place in the universe, especially at the present time, has to do with the need to balance and rectify this weakness.

From one point of view this need is superfluous. Inner presence just *is*, unconditional and inviolate. And yet, we cannot deny the life, vibrancy and joy that connection with inner presence brings—nor conversely, the misery and desolation that we feel when this connection is absent.

We humans are relatively independent centers of consciousness. Yet the experience of inner presence indicates a need for a synergetic integration of "independence" (or "individuality") and "consciousness." When the Unity of Consciousness, or inner presence, permeates one's individual consciousness, one can be truly one's Self, the *sine qua non* condition for occupying one's place in relation to the different levels.

Seeing the Seeing

I wish to look into the nature of seeing, beginning with the distinction between seeing objects and seeing the seeing itself. It seems as if the former is clear and the latter mysterious, but it may be the other way around. The seeing of objects includes two phases: first, the seeing itself, and, second, the mental recognition of what has been seen.

Before looking at seeing I am faced with myself—as I am now. I understand that this is the starting point, but part of this starting point is an emotional objection to having to do this. Expressing this objection helps—something softens a bit. And as I keep looking at my state, I can include in it this action of looking.

Something interesting is revealed about the relationship between seeing and emotional tension (or refusal). As long as the tension is there, it is the terminus of the seeing, meaning the seeing can go no further. The tension blocks the view.

As if to prove the point, the tension subsides and the seeing becomes unobstructed. Phenomena are revealed as being transparent in the sense of being susceptible to evaporation under the influence of a concentrated attention.

I can certainly try to go further with this. Before I do, however, I feel the need to examine a feeling of dissatisfaction or unfulfillment that is present, despite my interest in the study of seeing. It is as if this study satisfies one part, leaving the need of another part unfulfilled.

Now I recognize the *mode* of the study of seeing as being oriented toward reaching conclusions. Thus the study is impure. Now something else appears: In seeing the dissatisfaction, I must choose between (1) identifying with it, or (2) remaining grounded in the impartial seeing. In case (1), the dissatisfaction is an annoying problem. In case (2), one part, at least, is free of the dissatisfaction.

Furthermore, as I keep looking impartially, the dissatisfaction weakens. The attention becomes related to another level. This leads to seeing the phenomena, the trees out the window, as being not only beautiful, but submerged in a truly infinite background.

This is fine. And yet, as soon as the attention changes back into its ordinary mode, the dissatisfaction returns. Now this dissatisfaction nags at me, calls for my attention. I recognize this dissatisfaction as a pattern that stems from an insatiable ego hunger—a hunger for A's, expressions of love, to "sit in front," etc. Can I now come to its core?

I am looking at this pattern in its nakedness. I see its quintessential personal character as well as the contrast between it and the impersonal beauty of the trees out the window. This pattern is the factor that keeps me captive in the personal realm!

I appreciate the clarity of this seeing. At this moment both the personal and the impersonal are present. Clearly, the nature of the personal pattern has not been fully uncovered yet—it hasn't lost its power. It is probably naïve to expect that it would—much more time with this question is needed.

Openness, Impressions, Self

Unexpectedly, the question, "Who am I?" appears freshly. In the light of this appearance I see that every impression I receive is covered up with subjective meanings that are derived from an unquestioned, tacit belief as to who I am. Hence the road to self-knowledge goes through subtraction—evidenced by the capacity to receive impressions as bare, unburdened by conditioned self. Through such barrenness the real meaning can shine. This was symbolized in the Old Testament as going through the desert before reaching the Promised Land.

Subtraction is a process, an ever-deepening one. I ask, "Who am I?" and feel that an underlying aspect of myself is in question. But who asks? And who receives the impression of the question? Who awaits an answer? The only meaningful step now is to delve again, beyond the subject/object mode, so that the question can go to work, as it were.

The idea of "self," like all ideas, is a hindrance. That is, unless one uses it merely as a jumping board, allowing the living experience to depart, radically, from the habitual response to the idea. But even as jumping boards, ideas and questions get tired. They lose their elasticity.

If one stops resonating with the question, "Who am I?", then it may be necessary to ask another question, such as, "What is the ground of existence?" One can probably affirm that any question, which by its very nature is unanswerable, will do. Search for Self is, on the face of it, an absurd occupation, as is the attempt to experience that which is the ground of existence.

As one continues to move in a direction that is rife with such manifest contradictions-in-terms, one can't help but break through into a new territory. "A new level of experience" is a name for the result of a transformation in the nature of experience. Inwardly, a new relationship within oneself emerges, and one is nourished by the depths of one's Self.

And what about the impressions of the outer world? How to understand them in relation to the newly opened depths of oneself? Something mysterious and wonderful happens once in a while, especially in relation to music. But, ordinarily, a certain dichotomy persists. A door remains closed. Staying in front of that door is the work of the moment.

The Mind of No Understanding

The idea that I am not this body–mind is not difficult to comprehend. Moments of seeing bring me to the point of uncertainty about who I am. Here, I vacillate between the seen (body–mind) and the openness—thereby coming upon a taste of nonidentification.

On the other hand, the expansion of mind to the point of both knowing and not knowing who I am is difficult. Furthermore, when this experience is approached, it becomes obvious that it cannot generate an appropriate trace in one's ordinary memory. The idea, "I am my absence," creates a mere non-understanding. Only when the mind of understanding quiets down, can the strange echo of this idea sound in oneself, however faintly.

And yet, when the wish to know who I am is experienced not as a force coming from me, but as an intelligence trying to reach me, everything changes. The experience becomes available at such moments without work, without effort, without preliminaries. I am walking along and all of a sudden I am shocked by the sensation that no one is walking.

At such a moment I know that the ground for remembering Self, or remembering no-Self, is a non-understanding mind, a mind of direct experience. As best I can tell, my awakening is the awakening of this mind, which floods the body–mind with invisible light.

The End of Mentation

The end of mentation is the end of self; self as a presumed center of awareness, which usurps the place of Self, the centerless field of awareness.

The jumping-off point is not a question of finding the right thought. It is a question of coming to be without thought, or maybe ceasing to identify with thought.

I am aware of the fact that what I am doing now is thinking, but the obvious paradox of thinking about the end of mentation does not bother me. It may well be the prerequisite for jumping off.

The crux of the end of mentation is really the end of the tight connection between attention and thought. Once this connection is severed, mentation will cease of itself.

In meditation, when I try to move toward stillness, I always see that the point is not to come to stillness in the sense of a center of awareness witnessing a blankness. But rather, the point is to come to stillness as the merging of subject and object, a transcendence of the subject/object mode.

And now I remember a quick moment in which I saw this clearly. I saw that in this transcendence, the eye can see itself. There is knowing by identity. This was expressed as follows:

"As I sat, watching the seer, then the seer of the seer, each became an object for the new subject. And by becoming an object ceased to be a seer.

As the infinite regress of seers 'collapsed' into the *real* seer, I understood the solution to the question, 'Can the eye see itself?' The eye cannot see itself as a subject looking at an object, but it can see itself in the identity of the knower and the known. Furthermore, this mode is the way of *any* seeing, except that ordinarily it is immediately followed by a division into a subject and an object, and this bifurcation happens so fast that it is mistaken for the seeing itself.

"This response to the question, 'Can the eye see itself?' does not solve the mystery of this self-seeing or in-seeing. This self-seeing is not of the mind and so does not lend itself to explication; even its memory stays as a memory of a mystery—the mystery of nonduality."

NOW AND HERE

A door has opened. As I enter, I am dazzled, and cannot see. I am

reminded of a part of a sentence from *Beelzebub's Tales*, ". . . as the blind

man said, 'We shall see.'"

Being connected to a center—I see desires there, without much force.

I see that they live on the rim of the circle surrounding this center.

In ordinary terms they may be strong and deep; in comparison with the

center, however, they are infinitesimally shallow—or the center is

infinitely deep.

> —*A Movement Toward the Center,*
> *page 69*

The Magical Moment

The moment I become aware of awareness is a threshold moment. I am present to both self and Self. There is small self, in whatever state it happens to be, and there is the conscious seer, who is present from the noumenal side. And then, there is something else—that third element that is entirely unobjectivizable, and yet its presence can be known. The makeup of the magical moment requires not only the presence of all three elements, but also the awareness of this presence.

The third element. When it is made known to me, at this moment, for instance, I feel as if I have returned home. I feel grounded without being grounded in anything. I am here—but here is no-place, and, of course, I am in Now, knowing that I am always in Now, and that at other times I am not in touch with this fact.

The paradox is that this profound change in state can come only when there is no wish whatsoever for a change of state.

I am awake when I am aware of this third element being present—in whatever is taking place. It is always the source of the awareness, but now, in a moment of awakening, it permeates this field in addition to being its source. Without this presence, there is a feeling of alienation. This or that is happening, and I may even be aware of these happenings, but—so what? There is no guide, no reason to go right rather than left. With the presence of Self, the situation is reversed: There is a tacit substratum of meaning no matter what is taking place, and no matter whether one turns right or left, although, at the same time, one seems to know which way to turn.

This experience clearly reveals that allowing ego to be in control is a mistake. Ego is seen as the usurper of Self, the servant who sits on the king's throne. All it can provide is the illusion that all is as it should be. By connecting with Self, I can see the ego as it ultimately is—as a generator of meaninglessness and unhappiness.

The appearance of Self was not and cannot be initiated by the one who tries for it. This appearance took place when I was paying attention to the field of awareness, that is to say when the attention was oriented toward the inner world. This reorientation is up to me. The appearance of Self is not.

On Being Here

I am here, relatively awake. My being here is not a statement of location in space. It has an absolute quality. It says, "My attention is with myself. The body is an aspect of this self. Hence, being here, where my body is, is an aspect of being here, with myself."

I am here, grounded in Self. The more grounded I am, the more indifferently I receive impressions—and the more marvelous the world of impressions becomes.

In this state of relative openness, how am I choosing my way? Toward which impressions do I direct the attention? "Here" is a complex, rich place. I am here, but *how* am I here? How is this determined, moment by moment?

As I look, I become aware of the two currents: an ordering principle, directing traffic whenever the noise subsides, and the entry of noise and distractions. I see this. But now, at this moment, I wish to penetrate more deeply into the atemporal process. I wish to see how the direction of the attention, and even the attention itself, arises from this central principle. When the awareness is choiceless, how do I choose?

What is the source of the question? The question is a way of trying to look inwardly, deeply. And the wish to look is an expression of the wish to be inwardly connected. But because the looking is directed by the question, the mental component is too strong. Still, the question is a way of coming back, again and again, to the cusp, the interface between the noumenal and the phenomenal worlds.

The more I look, the more I feel that this interface is the key to the mystery and creativity of Self, the door to the knowledge of who I am.

What Does It Mean to Be Here Now?

I

I look out the window, paying attention to the branches of a tree moving in the wind. To see anything moving, especially something as complex as a tree, is to see a myriad of changing relationships among the branches and leaves of this tree relative to other trees and other objects. But the experience of perceiving this tree has another dimension as well. I enter into a relationship with *this* tree, receiving its being. And if every action is reciprocal, the tree receives my being through the fact that my attention rests on it.

Having written the last paragraph, I see an issue here that calls for consideration. I am saying that every act of perception is, by its very nature, dualistic—that it involves a dualistic choice. Either I begin to think, and the issue of concern is the network of relationships, or the concern is with the *being* of that which I attend to—or both.

Even if an act of perception involves both modes, this understanding of perception is not to be the last word on this subject. The mistake seems to be taking the world to be a world of distinct items. As opposed to what? As opposed to *experiencing the One at the center of every experience.*

The phrase "experiencing the One" is self-contradictory. "The One" cannot be experienced as something that is distinct from the experiencer. There is something in what I am trying to indicate that cannot be conveyed by language.

Is "Be here now" the most we can say?

No. It is possible to speak of a state that transcends duality. Merrell-Wolff's expressions, "consciousness without an object," and "the attention being directed toward its source" do it.

Is it possible and desirable to aim toward a state of nonduality in one's sitting meditation practice, by invoking these ideas? Since the invocation itself is dualistic, while its aim is to reach nonduality, the invocation, having indicated to the attention how to direct itself, should be let go of.

II

I am sitting in front of the computer screen, trying to look at myself. I see that I am distracted by turning thoughts. I continue to look at myself, just as I am. Now I am aware of the tensions in the body. Now—of the suffering that these distractions and tensions create by preventing me from being open to a higher current.

I maintain awareness of how I am. Awareness of the state of the body deepens. I feel that it is important to continue to sense the body, and allow the suffering to be present in the field of my awareness. Now there is some awareness of the background of the tensions. It is important not to force anything—in any case, the presence I wish for cannot be forced.

As I continue to look, the question arises—what is this presence I wish for? And how is it different from the presence that is here now? There is something in the background of the tensions that transcends categorization as entity or nonentity; it is a kind of "empty presence." I continue to just let it be. My only action is looking. I see that the looking is of two kinds, a looking at the mental construct and a looking at what is now. The latter is empty of anything that can be described.

I see a connection between the two kinds of looking and the two kinds of identity—self and Self. Small self looks in a way that aims at seeing some thing. Big Self just looks. And naturally continues to maintain openness, emptiness, no-thing-ness, as I (Self) observe.

A Movement Toward the Center

As I sat in meditation this morning the following question arose. As I try to look in, into Self, into the unobjectivized, what is the place that I look from? As soon as the question arose I saw that at that moment I was looking from ego. And I remembered the experience of real seeing as "I am seen," rather than "I see." I remembered the spacious, non-ego place from which one sees anything, from which any impression is really received. And now, as I write this, another piece of the puzzle falls into place—accompanied by feelings of melting and of gratitude that attest to the fact that this is an insight. This non-ego place from which the inward exploration begins, will, most likely, be transcended. And it will be transcended because there can be no "place" at all, ego or non-ego, from which to look in. Looking in from any fixed place creates the subject/object dynamic, in which the object that is seen can't be the non-objectivized aim of the exploration. The distinction must be made between a unitive experience, an indescribable flash, and the experience of the very next instant, in which its vivid memory is tasted by "me."

I see now that the paradox of the search is that it must occur in the unitive mode, in the mode of unknowing. Otherwise it is an ordinary search for an ordinary item, conducted through the mind and within its domain. As long as there is a search, then, as I understand it, the search is misguided. Only at the moment that seeking is truly given up, can a real search begin. "I" cannot look in. "The other" does not know how either, but he can search for a way.

There is a growing wish for the experience of the One. As I follow my experience, there is a place where the most meaningful aspect of it is simply the fact that it is dualistic, that I, as subject, am watching a flow of objects on an inner screen. And then a wish arises to move to a unitive mode, one that I have tasted often, but only for short times. There is a growing wish to live there.

At this moment, I am aware of being connected to and fueled by this other level. It is precisely this that pulled me toward this writing to begin with, and is linked now with a sensation at the center of the body. Now: I am energized in this center, which is the grounding for the unitive mode. Simultaneously, there is a watching from the subject/object mode. If, however, I persevere in this kind of watching, a certain staleness creeps in.

I am aware, at *this* moment, of another mode of awareness—one that permeates its subject and is one with it. It requires paying attention, while giving up knowing in the ordinary sense of the word.

A door has opened. As I enter, I am dazzled, and cannot see. I am reminded of a part of a sentence from *Beelzebub's Tales*, ". . . as the blind man said, 'We shall see.'"

Being connected to a center—I see desires there, without much force. I see that they live on the rim of the circle surrounding this center. In ordinary terms they may be strong and deep; in comparison with the center, however, they are infinitesimally shallow—or the center is infinitely deep.

This is a powerful image. Rooted at the center, nothing is threatening. Nothing is powerfully alluring. There is, at most, a bending toward the desired object, or away from a condition of displeasure, like a reed bending in the wind. Rooted, it bends, but it can't go anywhere, it will not be carried away by the wind. The tragedy of ordinary life is one of being continually swept away by fears and desires. Being in this deep, desireless condition is so strange to feel. Because desires and aversions are the essence of being "me," and ego's *raison d'etre* is to promote them. An "I" that desires nothing? Why is it there—or rather, here?

The mystery of being and the mystery of becoming...becoming is not the moving toward being...how are the two related?

Being is in love with the creations of time, out of its infinite abundance. Giving to that which perishes, its giving is seemingly wasted. Yet, in reality, nothing is wasted. This giving starts a circulation—and atoms of the Absolute permeate the flow, suffusing becoming with being.

Being in Now

Being in now is being in transcendence. What is called "being in now," when "now" is a part of time is never *really* being in now, since now has no duration, it cannot contain contents for awareness. Hence, whenever I am aware of something, I am really aware of the past. But there is a possibility of really being in the now: All contents are removed and now expands into a domain to which measurements do not apply.

I see that I need spaciousness in my relation to the inner world, so that I am not taken over by the loudest voice I hear—so that I can listen to the voice of truth in me, which is weak. By "the voice of truth" I don't necessarily mean a voice that tells me the deepest truth; it can be as simple as a voice that urges me not to do something I am about to do.

So, right now I am giving myself this spaciousness, and I am looking. I see tensions that are related to desires. They manifest in this spaciousness like knots. Is it possible to transform their energy toward transcendence? I see the danger of trying to do this, of a doing that is directed by thought. So I just keep looking.

There is an opening in the background. The mind tries to understand and define; it cannot. At this moment, I see the two aspects—the dissatisfied ego and the transcendent. I see clearly that ego will never be satisfied. But I don't have to be identified with it.

Well, this can be put to the test right now. Because I feel a keen sense of dissatisfaction, I feel it poisoning the mind. There is, however, another "I"—an I who is not dissatisfied. This "I" is empty and open, able to derive meaning from simple things, like a plant I am looking at. I don't take sides, but allow the light of awareness in. At this instant, who am I? I feel myself as an unknown.

Whatever I see cannot be changed. But the flow of seeing energy can be relaxed and expanded. In other words, the intention to relax can be fruitfully directed toward myself.

The appropriate inner posture, then, is to watch whatever appears as if I am watching a movie (an attempt to change a movie is absurd!) while having, at the same time, an open, relaxed, unobstructed attention. This kind of work at relaxation is bound to affect the body and mind. Indirectly, it relaxes them. It is an indirect way toward their relaxation, as well as toward more openness in the flow of the attention.

Because this moment is different, I am aware now of the extent to which my ordinary attention is directed toward (outer and inner) objects. This is identification: the awareness of objects *without* the awareness of the space in which they arise or the attention that sees them. And, at this moment, I am also aware of the hunger, the natural need for having space for the subjective side—to be free of being glued to objects. In this moment, I am glimpsing the experience of just being—no subject, no object. As I do, the body becomes naturally relaxed.

In the past few weeks I have been plagued by a feeling of meaninglessness, which manifests in an occasional low feeling. And just now as I was heading for the computer, motivated by the wish to explore this feeling, I noticed that it was gone. In its place was a connection to awareness. This simple observation demonstrates the truth of William Segal's statement that we suffer from lack of relationship with a higher energy *that is always present*. The connection with this higher energy manifests as the state of being aware. When I am aware I feel connected to a larger space. I expressed the state of being aware just now by the phrase "having a connection with awareness." This is a good way of looking at this. Awareness is like a field of light which is always here. Being aware is being connected to this field.

Right now I see myself trying to use this understanding to guarantee that I will not suffer from meaninglessness anymore. The mind is doing what it was designed to do! And I also see a kind of response to this mental impulse, an understanding that because what is required is openness, cultivating this state cannot be reduced to an item on the mind's list of things to do or not to do.

At this moment I clearly see what evaded me before. The feeling of helplessness in the face of meaninglessness and depression, the feeling that no matter what I do, it doesn't help—comes from the attempt to find meaning on a personal level, through something that the ego can latch on to as an achievement. The fact is, none of these "achievements" can satisfy the hunger for the inner connection—the connection with a higher energy that is really a connection with the inner Self. By contrast, the experience of awareness erases the feeling of meaninglessness, because it satisfies this innate hunger.

And something else appears in this context. Ordinary meaning is connected with a mental structure. It is something I know and understand. But the awareness that is related to Self is meaningful in a much larger sense because it provides the beginning of an answer to the question, "What am I here for?"—without the need for a mental structure that explains why being aware is my rightful role in the universal drama. The experience of fulfillment proves that it is. At some future time, in an hour or a decade, I may have an explanation that is grounded in a paradigm. This will be good, but secondary. The cultivation of awareness is independent of such explanations.

Groping Toward Timelessness

I

It is Sunday morning, December 28, 10:34 a.m., and yet it is truly no time. I listen to the slight noises around me—this old house is full of them—and each one wakes me up, carries me away from space and time coordination. Now impulses of the inner world—slight feelings, fragments of thought—demand my attention. Each one, as it is, is all there is. Each one's essence is not commensurable with its mental designation.

So, the way to the center is wide open. When thoughts try to encompass and manipulate it, this way does seem narrow, difficult, impossible—the eye of a needle. The most difficult thing in this whole spiritual endeavor is to understand that *just as I am, I am already there—or rather, here.*

As soon as this truth is formulated, the mind rushes in to exploit it. Naturally, its meaning recedes; the formulation is in danger of becoming just a slogan for cheap sentimentality. But in reality, its truth is not defiled.

The idea of work...of effort...it gets me nowhere close to the mark unless the adjective "effortless" is added to it. Otherwise it is sheer stupidity. The persistent hallmark of my efforts is a tensing. The tensing used to be coarse; now it is subtle. But tensing it is—how could that be related to the drops of water sliding down the windowpane?

II

In a moment of real looking, a moment of clear perception, there is no "I," except the totally subjective. Logically this is so obvious, yet I am startled by the power of the experience.

Logically, the "I" is, by definition, the subject, and again by definition, the subject cannot be perceived (cannot be an object). But experientially, this simple statement is blurred by a haze of confusion between seeing and recall, between perception and conclusion, between simultaneity and time lag. Amidst this confusion, the phenomenal self comes to be seen as "I," because the idea of a self is confused with perceptions of thoughts and feelings. When one's house is clean, "I" is nowhere to be found.

This much is clear enough. Is it the last word about "I"?

In a moment of real seeing something is happening that is beyond the subject/object mode, though connected to it. One feels, and is, rooted in a background of sparkling subtlety, and out of this background the objects of perception emerge.

In a sense, such moments are enough. Wanting more is greed. In another sense, such moments beckon one to something other than themselves. What is that?

There is a growing sense that one is called to reverse one's understanding of what is real. From the ordinary point of view the objects of perception are real. The phenomenal world serves as one's frame of reference. Perceptions of a different order are, then, an invitation to another mode of being. Taking them in the ordinary mode leads to greed for more.

Clearly, I am groping. But I am groping, it seems, in the right territory. When ordinary conflicts and strivings quiet down, a deeper kind of genuine wishing can be present. Having no object, it can follow its own course.

Being Awareness Itself

I begin with sitting here, feeling how I am—and inject into the experience the knowledge that it will change. I will at some not-so-distant future time, feel very good. Amazing how difficult this notion is to accept! With the head I know it to be true, yet emotionally I am identified with feeling low.

Now, perhaps as a result of my attempt to know that the bad feeling will not last, I experience the unpleasant sensations without identification and without justification. I am as I am.

So, I keep looking, and the issue becomes the deepening of the looking. I see the unpleasantness, and also its neutral background. Now there is an opening at the bottom of the spine; some feelings arise. And I see a choice. Either use all this energy that is now available to escape the unpleasantness, or keep looking into the deep.

Just like Aristotle's sphere of stars that keep circulating out of love for the Prime Mover, I need to come to the point of keeping my attention undistracted, directed inward, out of love for God. Ego motivation, ambition, decision—none of these will do. At this moment I feel a softening of the emotions, some openness. As I look at myself, I clearly see that the pattern I usually call "self" is transient, not real self but rather conditioned self. There is something else underneath. I come anew to the question of wishing to see my awareness.

As I open more in the feelings, I realize that this opening is essential for being with the question. In order to contact it, I must be open to the point of emptiness.

Now I see that I can transcend the conditioned self by looking—but when I am back at its level I am back to it, with all its attendant discomfort, unpleasantness and so on.

Anyhow, right now I feel attraction to the question of seeing awareness, attraction to *being* awareness itself.

Awareness and Attention

I try to follow the attention very simply. I look around. All of a sudden it becomes clear that the light of consciousness is always present—every act of ordinary seeing requires it—and that through identification I deprive myself of the experience of this light.

—*The Source of the Attention, page 87*

Awareness, Attention, Impressions

I

Negative aspects of one's life, such as boredom, can be seen as expressions of the hunger for "the other." For example, when I find no interest in any project suggested by the mind, this refusal can be interpreted as saying, "I want something else. Everything you propose comes from self-image. I want to break away from that." Snatches of an internal debate become almost palpable:

—"But the refusal is a part of what keeps me imprisoned in self-image!"

—"Unless you become aware."

With the arising of this insight I begin to be aware of an opening into a formless region. I see that awareness in the subject/object mode is a confrontation between a fine intelligent energy (the attention) and a mental construct it cannot penetrate. Thus, the subject/object mode has the structure of an impasse. By contrast, in-seeing is the suffusing of the *process* of mental constructing with this fine energy, generating the experience of opening.

II

What is awareness, what is attention and what is the relationship between them?

I see awareness as a transparent, receptive background, and attention as a dynamic channel through which impressions reach awareness.

The capacity to experience, to be aware of impressions through the vehicle of attention is the gift of being sentient. It is an ultimate good—surpassing the relative value of the content of experiences. For man (in contradistinction to other sentient beings) there is an additional unique gift: the potential to awaken and become *aware* of this capacity. It is the identification with the content of the experiences that leads to the forming of preferences (pursuit of pleasure and avoidance of pain). And it is these preferences that obstruct the free-functioning interplay between awareness, attention and impressions.

The Constant Root of All Experiences

I

The snow has just stopped; through the window, a spectacular white view. Once in a while a small avalanche as the breeze shakes the heavy branches. As the wind subsides, the scene becomes one of perfect stillness, perfect beauty, accentuated by a few tiny flakes, hovering and slowly descending.

The awakened stillness is an energized one. It presumes a stirring of energies, a stirring that comes about through conscience or love.

II

Why is it that acute attention to sense impressions connects one to the noumenal dimension?

When I attend to myself listening, I attend to Self—and to the mystery of this nameless, timeless Self receiving impressions.

Intuition and real feelings relate one to both the eternal and the time-bound. The mind of contrasts and distinctions recognizes them as transient, and their timeless source becomes known as well.

Any experience, in itself, is eternal. It is only when the attention is not on the impression itself, but rather on the mentation it triggers, that the experience seems time-bound. In reality, it is not. Even the experience of thought, as an experience, is eternal.

But don't experiences come in succession, and isn't this succession what we call time?

As I look inward I discern sameness at the root of all experiences. Filtered through the mind that presumes time, this is perceived as a constant in time. But the mind that presumes time is not really separate from its source, the timeless mind. In fact, it is the presence of acute attention that connects the two. Looking more deeply, the "constant" meets with and dissolves into an eternal openness. This is as far as my experience goes. I suspect, however, that as this exploration deepens, the many, which are the surface aspects of the One, will still be there—but not necessarily in succession. The sense of succession is merely an arrangement imposed by the mind that presumes time.

Intuition and real feelings are true. Their truth is their oneness—to be true is to be rooted in the One. Hence, the deepest part of intuition and feeling is always the same.

III

Perhaps under the influence of the Christmas feeling, this morning during meditation, I felt that elements of my inner world are redeemed by being seen. I experienced impatience and looking at its source, an insight came. The source of this impatience is an active element in my world. When unseen, it is submerged in the unconscious—unformed, blind, and destined to always stay the same, like the condemned souls in Dante's inferno. When seen, it may stay unformed, but by being in touch with consciousness, it becomes an impression—and is thereby connected with the eternal, transformed and redeemed.

The Source of the Attention

I wish to let the attention move freely, and see, just see what takes place.

The crux of the search is already evident from this statement. Who wishes? And how can the wish permeate the next few minutes?

I see that the level of the wish is, at best, the level of ordinary attention—and not a level that can see this attention.

Now the feelings are touched, and, for a moment, the pure light of seeing is present. I see, and I don't know what I see. Or rather, I see the light and don't know what I see *by* the light.

I try to follow the attention very simply. I look around. All of a sudden it becomes clear that the light of consciousness is always present—every act of ordinary seeing requires it—and that through identification I deprive myself of the experience of this light.

Is it possible to penetrate to the source of the attention?

The question is fresh. As I look, however, old patterns keep coming. Can I let them go and not lose touch with the new element?

Now I see what the new element is. It is the absence of a wish for an experience that answers the question. It is the absence of a wish for closure.

The new element knows itself to be eternal. It lives in an atmosphere of open presence. For it, the tension of opposites is the medium of life, not a problem that must be resolved.

Now I see the question, "What is the source of the attention?" as a source of life, never to be answered in the way I expected when I first posed it.

A Crossroads of Possibilities

Every moment is a crossroads of possibilities.

The entity (or nonentity) that I call my "inner nature" is starved for impressions—for a special kind of impression, the impressions of self-consciousness. Therefore, when I remember myself, it is deeply satisfying for this inner nature. The taste of this satisfaction is the taste of returning home. And when I am asleep, it suffers.

A glimpse of myself asleep brings with it a taste of being wasted, of spending myself, of passive submission to unknown forces. By contrast, when I am home, *I can choose* to spend myself—for example, by giving some of my energies to help others.

When I am under the influence of desire, I spend my energies in the usually vain hope that satisfaction will come back to me. When I am in a state of identification, I lose my energies choicelessly—the identification becomes a channel through which my energies are sucked away, to end, I suppose, at the moon.

That's why the rightful activity of a man is remembering himself. Self-remembering is an appropriate action at the appropriate point—blocking the channel of identification and turning the attention and energy back toward oneself.

In a state of desire, the attention follows in hot pursuit of impressions. The latter, when "captured," are manipulated to serve that desire. Identification closes down altogether the channel that receives impressions. By contrast, in a state of self-remembering one's organism is open to receive the impressions as they are, interact with them and incorporate them appropriately.

When the attention is at home, receiving impressions, the experience is enriching rather than limiting. An attention that stays at home is like a welcoming host. Of course, there may be times when we choose to disengage from outer impressions and turn the attention toward its unobjectivized source. This is an opening to another level of impressions altogether—an opening to another reality.

A Source of Suffering

The meditation this morning was good. And now, as I pause to write, I feel the inner connection again. Through the center of the body there is a connection with the subjective.

Recent insights include seeing that the switch from subject/object seeing to in-seeing is a change in the type of attention, a matter of tuning in to a subtle attention that is present in in-seeing all the time. This also forms the background against which ordinary attention is seen.

As the attention opens, the objective field of view expands and deepens into the subjective. Furthermore, there is a recognition that the distinction between the two is maintained by the discriminating mind.

As I feel a relaxation at the center of the body, I see the need for melting, which is beginning to happen. Melting of the ego structure. An acute attention is aware of the subtle level that underlies the one I am ordinarily aware of. What it sees is beyond words.

Now I am attempting to let go of descriptions, of knowing through formulating.

I sat, trying for a few minutes. The attention came and went, and I became aware of the fact that the state that lies in waiting for the attention is one of vague dissatisfaction and desire, rather than a desire for a definite something. I wish to look at that state, which is present now. There is a sensation at the center of the body, as well as a feeling of lack, which generates a movement outward, as if to relieve it—except that nothing in the objective world can relieve it. So here we have a clear source of suffering, exacerbated by trying to relieve it in the wrong way. The transition from a clear awareness of wanting to this movement outward masks the wanting, which keeps simmering underneath.

This is quite a discovery! I am trying now to stay with the wanting and the sensation. Just that. The sensation is expanding. The wanting changes to a longing. A sensation in the chest appears. I realize that I take it for granted that wanting means wanting *something*, and I'm endlessly trying to find that something. What I actually see is just wanting—wanting without an object.

This feeling or sensation is an attractor for the attention. The attention does open up, and even becomes empty, but it seems to be called back, by this attractor that prevents it from really taking off into the unobjectivized.

The Integration of Attention and Awareness

Explicit thought is the *outcome* of awareness and is very different from awareness itself. The attention is called to the birthplace of thought. Attention that *dwells on thought* stays locked on the by-product, missing the experience of awareness itself.

The approach to consciousness is through *the integration of awareness and attention*. When the two fuse, they are transformed and the light of consciousness dawns.

One aspect of self-remembering is the call for the attention to remember the awareness. Awareness is (in part) the awareness of impressions, but not in their objectivized form. Rather, in the form of their entry to the organism as packets of energy. Hence awareness, receiving impressions, stays formless—like an ocean that can receive into itself, without being changed by that which it receives.

Ultimately, the continuum of the awareness is the source of the attention. Hence, when attention reunites with awareness a circle is closed. This may be the circle whose center is everywhere and whose circumference is nowhere. But phenomena radiate out from this center, into the dimension of definiteness, where their lives end as soon as they are created.

They survive through their influence on awareness, attention and other phenomena.

When attention and awareness are integrated, the person can be a channel for the energy of consciousness.

Through phenomena, the attention can find its way back to awareness itself, by looking for that which feeds it. Ultimately, phenomena are merely evocative. Being caught by them is our prison.

To keep things in perspective, the unification of awareness and attention is merely a beginning. Through the dynamic stillness of this unity, indescribable new levels of being can become accessible.

SUBJECT AND OBJECT

In openness I am sensitive to the "I am-ness" that lies at the heart of every impression. The sound of a car passing by says, "I am." So does the texture of the piece of wood in front of me. The sound and the texture *are*, and only we humans have the capacity to recognize this. With this gift comes the capacity to imitate such recognitions—the capacity to be false.

—*Truth and Falsity, page 120*

Subject and Object: An Exploration

Yesterday there was a moment when the question appeared, "Can I experience the very nature of experiencing?" The question came with a feeling of dizziness, an echo of which reappeared as I wrote the question just now.

This sort of question can only be answered through total awakening, since, in relative terms, it does not make sense. The accompanying feeling of dizziness was an indication of the nature of the question—as well as its potential.

The question is related to the unity of subject and object. Trying to experience this unity, I notice that *I am reluctant to give up the subject.* I hang on to something that has a familiar sense of "I." Of course, this something is itself merely a mental construct, a subtle object. It must be given up if the unity of subject and object is to be realized. Such a realization, like experiencing the nature of experiencing, is a leap to a presently unknown (though not unglimpsed) level.

With all that understood, can I approach the question now?

First, I see that, at this juncture, ordinary thinking is no help. Ordinary thinking, by its very nature, keeps one on the level of the many. What then, is the nature of this attention—the one that can perceive the unity of subject and object? In other words, if the illusion of the separateness of subject and object is a function of the attention that receives impressions, is there another attention, one that brings about a unitary experience?

As I watch myself confront the question, I see the attention beginning to enter a unitary mode, an unknown domain. I expect, however, that this will be but a brief excursion, and the attention will emerge from it with an answer in the domain of the known. Having expressed that, I realize that the opposite is the case. The question can be a lure to the unknown. And the excursion, if successful, has the potential to transform.

Beyond this understanding glimmers another. All these concepts and images, from *excursion* and *unknown*, to *brief* or *long* miss the mark. That which I am beginning to faintly experience right now is outside their scope. And to the extent that they set up expectations, such as a long excursion or a brief one, they lead me astray by directing the attention to follow a description.

The depth of my experience at this moment is, indeed, indescribable. If I am pressed for a description, Tulku Urgyen's expression, "empty cognizance" comes to mind. He said, "Empty cognizance means that while mind is basically empty, it still cognizes. What people usually do is they understand only one of the two aspects: that it's empty and they hold unto that, or there is knowing and they hold unto that. This is called lacking the view of unity. And unity means that the mind in essence really is empty, and at the same time, naturally, there is knowing."

That part of the attention that connects the experience with a description affirms the veracity of Urgyen's description. Still, this only means that this description is the best projection of the experience onto the lower level of thought. Essentially, the experience itself remains indescribable.

In saying that the experience of this moment is indescribable I am not saying that it answers the question. This experience has to do with the unity of the subject and object, but the issue is still here. I wish to approach it from the other direction—looking, without interference, at the functioning of the dualistic subject/object mode.

Here, the element that stands out is a feeling of time delay. The objects I experience are of the past, the immediate past to be sure, but past nonetheless. In this sense they are dead—not a part of the living present.

Additionally, there is a puzzle here: if subject and object are separate, then what connects them?

I hear the ticking of a clock and let go of thinking about subject and objects. Instead, I listen. Listening intently, I discern a structure within each tick, but this structure is not experienced in the same way that a whole tick is heard. It is discerned in an "empty" sort of way. More generally, the hearing of a sound as sound seems to be but a crust, covering an experience in which the sound is first received as no-sound. This observation seems to touch on the domain where the relationship between the dualistic and the unitary modes of receiving impressions can be explored.

Noumena and Phenomena

Phenomena can be described.
Noumna can be expressed.
Phenomena are the expression.

I

I feel the enormity of the call for freedom from the phantasmagoria of the phenomenal world. This freedom can only be arrived at by discovering that which is more real than the phenomenal as well as by seeing the true nature of the phenomenal—especially the fact that it lacks independent existence.

This possibility can be theoretically appreciated by ordinary thinking; it cannot be experienced by that which underpins ordinary thinking—the ego. I can theoretically appreciate the phantasmagoric character of the phenomenal world, but, perceptually and emotionally, it remains solid.

The proposition that this solidity is but an illusion points toward "something else," something whose enormity is incommensurably greater than that of the physical universe. So much greater is this "something else" that it can support the appearance of the phenomenal world without being diminished by it in any way—just as my psyche is undiminished by the production of dreams.

As I write, I feel a presence, associated with a sensation at the center of my body. This presence points toward this *something else*, but it does not confront the sense of reality that I associate with the world of objects around me. The two worlds exist in me side by side. One is Life itself; the other is the world of appearances. Thinking about it in terms of the Law of Three, I see that I am called to be the third force, to bring about this confrontation.

The confrontation is not really a function of ordinary mind. It has to take place in the depth of the soul, where the production of the world of objects occurs in the dark. Hence the need for the deepening of "the inner connection."

Psychologically, a barrier to this confrontation is the sense of comfort and support (and the corresponding fear of their disappearance) that I derive from the phenomenal world. I do have glimpses of its insubstantial nature—by this I mean that when any aspect of it is examined with a keen attention, it just evaporates. But so far I have been reluctant to follow these glimpses.

Thus, the inner presence that I continue to feel has a blind quality to it. It does feed me, but *it does not confront its own real (unitive) seeing with the fragmented object–seeing of the ordinary mind*. Perhaps it is not only a question of direct confrontation. It may be also a question of letting the unitive mind live and participate in my life by following its perceptions— perceptions that appear as intuitions and spontaneous arisings, calls that can be trusted without knowing why.

II

A simple exercise: *stop* during ordinary, everyday functioning to give "the other" a chance to appear.

I see a hunger for something undefined, a hunger that is contaminated by free-floating anxiety, by fear-without-an-object, and also by a vague expectation of pleasure, the pleasure of anticipated fulfillment arising out of anticipated events.

As I watch the manifestation of all this in my body, I see something important. *The possibility of change stems from seeing in the unitive mode*: As I look at the manifestations of the body, I see myself looking in the subject/object mode—which really means looking at the mental image that was created (I don't know how) when I began to look. *Looking at this mental image fixes the state—and makes change impossible.* The fixation was released as soon as I allowed myself to delve, however briefly, into seeing in the unitive mode (in-seeing).

There is a dichotomy here. The mental images that arise in the subject/object mode seem to be clear. On the other hand, seeing in the unitive mode feels blind, yet nourishing. I'll delve into it a bit deeper. When I look inward, I observe the seeing rather than the content. Now, the contents are really separate from the seeing, just as a mirror is separate from that which is reflected in it. In-seeing is like a nonobjective seeing *of* the mirror. It is as if by cultivating in-seeing, I cultivate a relationship with the mirror itself, without paying attention to the reflected images.

The analogy between awareness and a mirror is a powerful one. It implies that, just as a mirror is an interface between real objects and their reflections, awareness is an interface between the unitive real world and its appearance as a multitude of separate entities in space and time. Perhaps the issue is not elimination of the phenomenal world from awareness (in favor of the awareness of the real), but rather seeing it all—the real, the phenomenal and the awareness, in their proper relationships.

What arises now is this. The struggle that I engage in while trying to transcend ordinary awareness feels wrong somehow. It is like trying to overcome an ill-defined barrier. This struggle places me squarely in an action–reaction dynamic, where a stronger action gives rise to a stronger reaction. Rather, the search should be about how to open, how to transcend struggling.

Looking Inward

Looking inward, I have a sense of "nothing looking at nothing." Nothing is seen, yet I am very much here. There is an opening in the lower part of the spine.

I continue to look and there is a back-and-forth shifting of viewpoint between object-seeing and this introception (the state of consciousness without an object). The return of introception is associated with a greater feeling of freedom. It feels as if there is a very large inner space that introception opens up.

Now there is some emotional awakening. The more grounded I am in introception, the more intense the feeling. Also, while it feels very satisfying to be here, it is clear that the feelings are extraneous to the state, clearly belonging to a more superficial level.

I discover that there is no need for the mind to deal with objects now. A state where objects are absent from the attention is much more satisfying. Furthermore, when the body is open and relaxed, as it is now, the introceptive state is there, in the background, and ready to emerge as soon as I cease thinking. It keeps coming, in spurts of short duration. The mental acknowledgment that it happened appears after the fact, after the spurt has ended. During such a spurt, consciousness has no content.

Looking at the superficial, I can feel the ego, a very small and limited sense of self. Regarding the introceptive state, however, there is another point. Sometimes the state itself seems ungrounded. (I am not sure what I mean by this; there is a feeling that it could kind of float in the abyss. I am trying to express in words something for which words are inadequate.) In reality, however, the introceptive state is completely grounded, and the ground is precisely the Self. Furthermore, it is an absolute ground (unconditioned and unconditionable).

As I continue, the state varies, first deepening, then giving way to thought. It feels as if a door is wide open; sometimes I am on one side of it, sometimes on the other. The opening is the emptiness in consciousness.

In Search of Self

I am sitting here, watching myself—observing once again, the intrusion of thought and the presence of tensions. Now I also am aware of a sensation along the spine, a sensation that makes the spine a kind of *axis mundi* of the microcosmos of myself. Emotions arise in conjunction with the tensions. It is almost as if the separation between emotion and tension is due to the mind's way of analyzing things, and does not correspond to a real distinction. At any rate, there is a real presence now, a presence that is grounded in this sensation in the spine.

As I continue to be aware of staying with this presence, a question arises: Who is the "I" that is staying with the presence? Clearly, mental responses to this question amount to an objectivation of this unobjectivizable "I." This will not do. If the question is to be confronted at all, it must be confronted by an attention that delves into the subjective domain.

Now there is the beginning of an unexpected feeling—a stirring of life, of gratitude, of a warmth superimposed on the presence. It is as if the "I" that is sought is beginning to respond.

This arising of feelings is hardly surprising. The question came from the cool, discriminating intellect. But the movement into the subjective domain is a movement away from distinctions and toward wholeness. Small wonder that feelings, which are not concerned with distinctions, arise.

I welcome the feelings, and, as I do, they become more pronounced. But—once again—who is the "I" that is welcoming them? What is the source of the impulse to welcome? Actually, these two questions are different. The source is the understanding that what is has to be accepted. This welcoming impulse is presented to "I," which mysteriously, initiates the action of acceptance.

This "I" is experienced now as the central still point of my being. It is doing nothing, yet without it—how is it possible to imagine life without it? If I try, expressions like "chaos" or "being eternally lost" appear. To be without this "I," or without the access to the experience of it, must be the experience of hell.

Needless to say, this central still point is not in space. Rather, it envelopes and permeates all of space, giving to whatever is the quality of is-ness or being. Attempts to arrive at descriptions of it fall flat. In fact, the very thought of it as an "it" is a separation from the truth.

A Tale of Two Mysteries

When one waits, *something appears.* As if to test this truth, I wait in front of the computer screen and a flow of subtle energy appears in the chest and abdomen, bringing with it softness and a warm feeling. At once I am faced with the mystery of my existence, as well as the (different) mystery of existence itself. My existence is existence itself—with the feeling of "I" added on. This is small self. The mystery of existence, however, is enmeshed in big Self.

The presence of this subtle energy brings me to an organic state of questioning. It is as if when expressed through Self, Existence itself seems to ask "Who am I?" While the Self that is the vehicle for this question is associated with this body–mind. And yet, it is entirely impersonal.

As I stay in this state, the mind becomes receptive to unusual thoughts and feelings. For example—the unfolding of the processes in nature is nature's own response to this question of "Who am I?" And my own unfolding serves the same purpose, except that in my case, a conscious presence of the question is possible (and takes place now). Furthermore, the addition of this element of consciousness is necessary and important.

This state of questioning contains both an element of unfulfill-ment (which is inherent to any question) and an element of deep fulfillment—the taste of being in the right place and asking, or rather being, the right question.

Clearly, as far as the question is concerned, the mind is irrelevant. It is allowed to know something of what's going on, but its function is to remind the attention to stay its course.

II

Now I am flooded with experiences that illustrate the two in me—the two natures.

At this moment the body is energized, senses alert. This experience is connected to a sensation of the background; there is a nothingness behind the body–mind, and the awareness now encompasses it.

Now something interesting is revealed. The mind, persisting in its dissatisfaction, is looking for something for itself, like a hungry dog looking for a bone. So at this moment, I feel the two natures—one is deeply content and the other is not.

It is somehow evident, at this moment, that this dissatisfaction is *the very nature of the mind*. The stiller I become, the more mute the dissatisfaction. The reason for this is clear. The stiller I am, the more open I am to Self, and it is the separation from Self that is at the core of the dissatisfaction. Mind, taking itself for a self-subsisting unit, tends to be self-enclosed, self-preoccupied and separate. It takes enlightened intention to first understand the situation—and then, to expand the attention, opening the mind to its vast background.

Some reflections on opening to Self.

Part of the difficulty of realizing who one is, is the difficulty in accepting the incredible freedom that accompanies the realization. At each moment *everything* is opened anew.

When I withdraw from the identifications of the moment, I find myself in the Unformed, which is Now=eternity. The challenge is to be in Now while being active in the world. This is what self-remembering is about. In self-remembering, the attention is open to forms; the vastness of the Unformed receives them. There is no grasping. Grasping, or attachment, is the mechanism whereby the attention becomes severed from its source. Rather than being as vast as an ocean, the attention becomes wrapped up in a wave, believing that this small wave is the totality.

self and Self

The ordinary sense of self is felt and seen as an object in front of the mind's eye. Of course, the self that is seen as an object is different from the self that is perceived as a thought–emotion complex—a complex that functions in the dark. But I can feel the relationship between the two. Something in me follows the process of objectivation, and confirms that the object I see is, in this case, a fair representation. The two are related—somewhat like the relationship between a film negative and the picture that is printed from it.

Real Self and self are very different. An intimation of Real Self can only come from the side of the Subject. After all, "I" am, first and foremost, a Subject. It cannot be approached from the objective side—Self can only be approached when one looks deeply into the Subject. By contrast, ordinary self is a pattern of thoughts and feelings that can be objectivized and examined without loss of essential features. The reason: this self is not really "I" at all.

The discovery of this difference between Self and self in relation to the process of objectivation is interesting not only in terms of content, but also in terms of implication: This discovery implies that *there is an attention that can be present to both sides, the objective and the subjective,* and this attention evaluates processes in both domains; it can be present even during the transition from one domain to the other. The subjective domain is hidden from the ordinary mind of contrasts and distinctions, but not from this attention. Furthermore, this attention is also connected with the mind—otherwise, how could I have written the previous paragraph?

At this moment I feel connected to both domains, the subjective and the objective. The feeling is one of expansion in both horizontal and vertical directions. Thoughts continue, but they take only a part of the space to which and in which I am present.

Through this experience the subjective domain is revealed as the foundation of the objective. When I am grounded in it, I can be present to the world of objects while in a relaxed, relatively still state.

An Open Search

When the search for who I am is conducted from the side of relative consciousness, the results are uncertain. In fortunate cases, there is transformation, an inflow from the side of absolute consciousness. But there is no way to initiate this happening from the side of relative consciousness. So, when I (ego) initiate a search, I must be oblivious to the idea of attainment. It needs to be, simply, an honest search.

When experiences related to this search are combined with a theoretical understanding, conclusions emerge. For example, I know that Self cannot be objectivized. Hence it cannot be an object of experience. Or, when it is experienced in the objectivized mode, what is experienced is not really It. What is the relationship between such understanding and the search as it proceeds in the moment?

When the search is ongoing, it exists on a number of levels, and its essential quality must be openness. Therefore any thought carried into the moment by the ego is in the way. One must trust that understanding operates without the ego's participation. Likewise, relative consciousness cannot know Self. And yet, as we have just said, the search must begin with relative consciousness. How is this apparent paradox resolved?

The point of the search, as it is conducted by relative consciousness, is not to find It, but to create conditions for It (absolute consciousness) to appear. Paradoxically, these conditions include an honest search. Such a search, through its inherent limitations, leads to the interface between the relative and absolute aspects of consciousness, that is, to stillness.

Stillness is not the opposite of search. On the contrary, real search requires a background of stillness.

As I quietly survey the body and follow the breath, the stillness deepens. I know that the attention that surveys the body and follows the breath cannot lead to awareness of Self. However, it is through sensing of the body and awareness of breath that the stillness deepens. A feeling of "I" arises, an "I" that is not separate from the impressions, a feeling of "I" that permeates the impressions that keep coming.

This experience, clear and wonderful as it is, is merely a hint. While one part of this "I" permeates what is perceived as outer, another part looks into an inner space of incredible depth.

Truth and Falsity

It is obviously false to say, "I am not." But can I truly say, "I am?"

I

I cannot possibly have a true feeling of "I am not." When I do, or rather believe I do, the feeling is actually an aspect of "I am."

Then why do I doubt the feeling of "I am" that appears now? If this doubt is valid, it is not because my "I am-ness" is in doubt, ever—but rather because the feeling "I am" does not originate from the source of its truth.

Paradoxically, the validity of this doubt is a bridge to the Experience. I am the source of both truth and falsity. The realization of either is a true expression of Self. But the identification with such a realization falsifies it in the sense of placing the attention on a dead image, or a memory, rather than on the source of the image.

II

As I read this passage, it feels as both true and false. It is true in terms of content, but false in the rigidity of expression—the words are true, but the music is false. The one who is good at theoretical formulations is not who I really am.

True beliefs, true statements dissolve now.

There is an open space in which nothing is false; it is just that some currents are truer than others. Even the so-called "false" is an expression of the truth.

I am at peace.

This is the beginning of openness.

III

In openness I am sensitive to the "I am-ness" that lies at the heart of every impression. The sound of a car passing by says, "I am." So does the texture of the piece of wood in front of me. The sound and the texture *are*, and only we humans have the capacity to recognize this. With this gift comes the capacity to imitate such recognitions—the capacity to be false.

IV

The recognition of the "I am-ness" at the center of every impression is the key that opens the gate to the experience of "I am," the Experience that transcends all experiences. The recognition of this "I am-ness" is passive; it comes when ordinary activities cease. Yet through the recognition, one comes to the truly active, the real doing, the authentic expression of "I am."

One need not say, "I am." One can say, "the flower is." Or one can just relax into the wonder of it all, and be this wonder. This recognition of "I am" in Self and in other, in every impression, is the role we are called to play in the drama that is the universe. It is our payment for the boon of enjoying the consciousness of who we are.

The essential feature of everything is that *it is*. Why not recognize this? If we recognize this unitive feature, then, paradoxically, the distinctive features, the differences in sounds, textures, colors, are even more clearly present to our awareness.

V

Parmenides knew this twenty-five centuries ago. He said, "Being is. Non-being is not. These are the only true statements we can make."

Affirming "I Am"

Descartes' "I think, therefore I am" is an *indirect* affirmation of existence, via a logical operation. It implies a trust in logic and in the mind's ability to perform logical operations correctly. Descartes' affirmation then, is not the direct experience of "I am," but rather the experience of thinking and of logical deductions.

By contrast, there is a way of directly experiencing "I am." But, discursively speaking, this experience can be rather puzzling. What is being affirmed, and how? The affirmation, "I am," is expressed in thought, but what is being affirmed is the entire subjective element that, as such, cannot be experienced by ordinary mind. Moreover, the certainty of the affirmation comes hand-in-hand with a paradoxical inability to elaborate on what is being affirmed. An inability that, from the point of view of thought, may be interpreted as vagueness and may even lead to a fading of the certainty.

The inability to elaborate is not necessarily inherent in the experience. It may merely indicate that while the affirmation "I am" is relatively accessible, the ability to stay with the experience as it deepens is not. And from the point of view of the experience itself, such elaboration may be unnecessary, anyway.

There is another riddle: Even if the capacity to experience one's existence as well as the capacity to think and express thoughts about that experience are accepted at face value, the relation between the two remains a great mystery. How does the absolutely subjective experience become transmitted, with a sense of certainty, to the mind—the instrument of manipulating objectivized entities?

A computer cannot affirm its existence. The experience and expression of such affirmation is possible through the *richness of different levels* in a unified field of attention. The simple, almost ordinary affirmation of "I am" is really the affirmation of the existence of one's *attention*; it is not the experience of subject as distinct from objects. In the experience of "I am," the attention turns inward, toward its own depth, and objects momentarily disappear.

Being In Touch With Stillness

I see that as an isolated entity I cannot be still. To be still is to participate in the stillness that is always here.

At this moment I feel good. The feelings are alive. I see that it is important, while accepting this, not to be identified with it. Ego is only too ready to appropriate these good energies for its purposes, and forget about the impersonal dimension.

I try to see, with great acuity, the actuality as well as the possibilities of this moment. I discern an inner shift, which is an aspect of being still—a shift away from being me, away from being anybody. To be me is to be a subject for an object, that is, to be a subject in the act of perception in the subject/object mode.

I feel that this idea brings me to the verge of an important discovery. I see that I cannot go after this new discovery with the mind. When I try to think about it, it recedes. I see that my stance now needs to be presence without the slightest interference, presence without intention for anything.

When I am not a subject for an object, when I am in a nondual state, *I am this nonduality*. I feel a bit uneasy about writing this. Is there a vestige of me in the making of this statement? Yes, it comes not only from the experience but also from prior understanding, from memory.

I experience now the reversal of active and passive that William Segal wrote about. The stillness has an active quality to it, it tries to enter me. My part is to be present and passive, to be here, doing nothing. This is very clear.

As I noticed before, after being in touch with stillness for a while, I feel invigorated, and ego is ready to come back and take charge. Whether this is lawful or not depends on the situation. It could be lawfully appropriate, and it could be laziness, reluctance to continue the very subtle effort of not interfering. This very subtle effort is needed. This is the jumping board, a step into the place of no-effort. This step cannot be taken by "me."

The way to nonduality begins with an either/or. Either I am open, still, attentive—or I am not.

What, then, is the way to *not* being a subject for an object? Is it the seeing of the bifurcation, the transition from a unitive mode of perception to a subject/object mode? Can this transition be seen so clearly that, naturally, non-doing takes place?

Is it possible to observe the moment of transition from the unitive mode of perception to the subject/object mode? Is it possible to see this bifurcation or splitting so clearly that I can choose not to do it?

Total Subjectivity

As I faced the question, "Who am I?" while remembering that "I" is irrevocably the subject, that the attention will never find it where it is accustomed to look (among objects), the attention turned inward—and all hope of finding an answer was gone. Instead of an answer, this reorientation of the attention brought about a *presence* that was grounded in the subjectivity of oneself. From this grounding, I saw that ordinarily I am oriented toward the outside of myself, toward my projections, which I take to be independently existing entities. I saw that this orientation weakens me and cannot lead to genuine fulfillment. By contrast, being firmly established in the "middle ground," the place of attending to both the subjective and the objective, is a remedy for the malady of feeling dependent on the happenings in the objective domain. Furthermore, I saw that this grounding is a natural result of the cultivation of stillness, and that, without it, the stillness is thin, easily disturbed. With it, the stillness is an aspect of who one is.

A few days later, further contemplation led to another insight. Rather than being merely one pole of the subject/object relationship, total subjectivity is a higher state, one that transcends both subject and objects, while giving rise to them by bifurcation. Trying to rely on objects for support is like relying on the movie pictures that are projected onto a screen. One needs to come back, again and again, to the place (or no-place) that is beyond both subject and objects.

These ideas led to still another experience. Listening to music, I became aware that I was receiving it in two distinct modes: I was hearing the music as a series of objectivized sounds, and behind that I was receiving the music as a quiet, energizing flow directly into the subjective domain. It felt at the time as if opening the gate for this flow was a matter of an inner shift, which could be initiated at will. Whether this is so remains to be seen. At any rate, I felt that by occupying the middle ground, as I did during this listening, I became the gate through which energies could flow from the outside (the sounds) to the inside (the domain of total subjectivity).

And how does all this apply to the issue of the personal and the impersonal? On one occasion of attending to this openness, the attending was understood as *giving up* experiencing as I know it—that is to say, giving up experiencing as if from a personal center, experiencing in the sense of "I am experiencing."

At that moment of openness, I clearly saw that release from thought is the precondition for being in the middle ground and attending as pure subject.

FINAL NOTES

Always, we only hear what we are.

—The Still Small Voice, page 144

Reciprocal Maintenance
of All and Everything

According to Plotinus, just as the Soul of the Universe enters all things to the end "that the total of things might be possessed by intellect," the soul of each one of us is sent to the body to govern it so "that the universe may be complete" (*The Enneads*, VIII, 1).

The bodhisattva way of life expresses a similar principle. Having gained the capacity to transcend the cycles of birth and death, the bodhisattva willingly participates in the cycles, bringing higher influences to the realms of the lower.

In Gurdjieff's expression of the laws of world creation and world maintenance, this principle is put into perspective through the account of the transition from the system "Autoegocrat" to the system "Trogoautoegocrat." A deep mystery at the heart of Reality requires that all things and all levels participate in and feed each other. An isolated entity, even the highest, cannot endure.

Now, it seems that the general intellectual climate of our era is one of readiness to receive a new insight. This insight comes through different, parallel channels—art, science, philosophy, literature. Science sets out to investigate reality by first truncating it, through objectivation, and then breaking it apart, through reductionism. So it is particularly significant that the aspects of wholeness, coherence and interpenetration of levels make their appearance in this arena.

Let us begin with Gurdjieff's assertion, "Everything is material." Everything is material, but what is matter? Quantum physics agrees with the Aristotelian view that matter as such is pure potentiality. Quantum physics further asserts that as pure potentialities (or "quantum systems"), material systems exist in isolation and in the mode of no contradiction between "is" and "is not" (they do not exist in space–time). This existence is coherent, perfectly deterministic, governed by order. For a system to interact with the rest of the universe, however, it must descend into the ordinary phenomenal existence in space–time. This descent into the "either/or" mode of existence in space–time is marked by unpredictability. The origination of this unpredictability is not well understood, even within the paradigm of physics, but an act of creation, whose origin is unknown, is involved. And it is clear that a subtle interplay between potentialities and actualities is the very fabric of the universe as we know it.

The analogy between the descent of matter into activity in the world, and the descent of the soul into the body, carries only up to a point. Matter *per se* is pure potentiality that is not aware of itself, while the essence of the function of the soul is to awaken an organism to an awareness of its potential. Likewise, the function of a bodhisattva in the world is to bring knowledge of an undreamed potential to people who are ignorant of it.

In fulfilling his function, a bodhisattva serves not only our needs, but also the needs of the higher: Knowledge is, in itself, pure potentiality. It too needs to descend and penetrate living forms, so "that the universe may be complete."

Toward the Middle Ground

I begin by looking at how I am now. There is a vague, somewhat remote wish for creative impressions. It is constrained, suffocated, though—simply by how I am. But as I look, there is movement.

The mind begins by looking at thoughts. Frustrated, it continues by looking among no-thoughts. A background of ineffable subtlety begins to reveal itself. The mind recognizes that in the perception of this background, its own nature as background is denied—the perception makes it into a foreground. So, the active mind recedes. This is a new level of unconditioned looking. Looking merges with just being, and it is a delight to be.

The thread is thin, and easily lost. But the possibility, discovered, cannot be denied. Here, the mind expands into the nondichotomous. As a certain element of control is given up, a release from deep conditioning takes place.

When in touch with this thread, I feel close to myself. Relaxation naturally sets in; the feelings are alive. Nothing is denied. Every impression is welcome.

And now I become aware that this condition—inhabiting the middle ground—is merely the surround of real activity. Perhaps the expression "effortless effort" is appropriate here. Deep energies are churned—and may appear and act if the field stays open.

Perhaps my part is just a vigilant noninterference, merely allowing. Certainly, it is not ordinary self, but a deeper Self that is called to do.

II

One of the outcomes of openness is an awareness of the actual field of invisible vibrations that surrounds, permeates and influences the visible. In openness, awareness is nongrasping, neither conditioned by nor leading to mental constructs.

It seems to me now that the relationship between the timeless reality of Self and the phenomenal world is to be found in this awareness, and that this awareness functions via real feelings. As indicated in Gurdjieff's food diagram, ordinary attention, a function of the intellectual part of ordinary mind, can be the link to the higher emotional center.

This understanding does not resolve the sense of puzzlement that arises with contemplation of either myself or the world around.

Reality does present itself as a puzzle. But this puzzle is a call for expansion of mind, for finding meaning at the center of meaninglessness. The sense of puzzlement must be transformed. What is the "meaning" we are looking for?

III

Now, as I sit here, the sound of a gentle rain creates a mellow, soothing influence, and a whole-body sensation brings a gentle balance to the feelings. Awareness, of itself, turns to a deeper layer, to the witnessing of process, to a kind of looking that knows that there is no thing to be seen.

The seeing of process brings me to the limits of my mental constructs. What is beyond them, what is revealed to a deeper seeing, is awareness itself—unlimited, unformed vistas, into which the awareness flows, and from which energy comes.

Being like this, I feel at home. The sounds of cello and flute that enter my awareness now are carried on cushions of feeling, on a background of indifferent attention. There is ample room for everything. The wrong notes are as interesting as the right ones.

I don't know who I am, but at this moment, I am not far from this Unknown. There is a taste of simplicity, and of at-one-ness with an invisible flow. When the inner connection, the in-seeing, wanes, there arises a reminder in the form of a hunger for it. Everything is here.

Receiving Impressions

I listen to the hum of the computer. Spontaneously, side-by-side with this listening comes an impression of spaciousness. Initially this spaciousness is received by ego—but then, something relaxes, and there is just spaciousness. The presence of ego is associated with slight tensions and is there as a "center-of-experiencing." Pure awareness of spaciousness requires no such center-of-experiencing.

Well then, can there be an awareness of sights, sounds, etc., in addition to spaciousness? I go back to listening to the hum of the computer. Again, relaxation comes. The situation is not as clear as before, but it seems that the recognition of the sound as "computer hum" is related to ego. Next, the spaciousness shifts from being *beside* the hum to being its background.

Now relaxation spreads through the body, together with the beginning of feelings. I let go of the wish to pin things down. But as I follow the relaxation, I can't help seeing that ego is present as well. I feel that this cusp between the presence and the absence of this center of experiencing is of monumental significance. Freedom, it seems, is precisely freedom from that center.

Pleasure is the satisfaction of ego. Joy is the absence of ego.

Well, then, how are impressions received? If they are received by ego, they are degraded by being categorized ("understood"), a process that takes the life out of them. If, however, they are received by spaciousness, they bring life to the organism, and a synergetic, joyous upgrading of the impressions and the organism takes place.

Bringing Order to the Formless

I

Each ordinary experience of "I" comes from a limitation in the penetrating power of attention. As I look inward, at a certain point I choose to look at what I see in the subject/object mode. The subject/object mode is *based*—split-second by split-second—on real seeing, which is participatory and unitive. Real seeing, prior to bifurcation or the splitting of what was whole into subject and object, is the beginning of freedom.

II

Ordinary mentation is always concerned with the limited: the needs of the body, the demands of the mind, desires, the project at hand. Its tyranny over attention is the barrier. When attention is allowed to be in touch with the formless, and be directed by Self, *its function becomes to bring order to the formless* ("Let there be light" on the primordial chaos).

Order in the phenomenal world is a by-product. Attention, integrated with awareness, does the work of bringing order to the unformed.

The idea of order in the unformed is not strange to a physicist. The unformed is the realm of potentialities. The term *quantum states* expresses exactly that—precise structure in the realm of potentialities. Momentary phenomenal appearances ("elementary quantum events") serve as shock points in the flux of fields of potentialities. They introduce unpredictable discontinuities into the smooth flow of these fields.

The bringing of order to the unformed is not the business of the phenomenal self. Of course, when phenomenal self is transcended, there is no problem. Even ordinarily, when it is unavoidably present, it need not be a hindrance. It is enough if it recognizes its place and yields. When it does not recognize its place, it comes in conflict with Reality, and confusion and suffering ensue.

III

I sit here, and, at this moment I don't need anything. Sitting here is enough. Conditioned impulses are tugging at my sleeve, feeling uncomfortable with my sitting here when there is much to do. But I am content just sitting here.

The little sounds the house produces are pregnant with meaning. Not ordinary meaning, which connects an event with past, future and function, but meaning that connects with inner dimensions. The depth of this meaning fluctuates, as my inner connections do. When thinking releases its hold, openness is here. When an experience triggers mental curiosity, the inner flow is blocked.

Relaxation deepens now to the point where even die-hard tensions are bathed in a background of relaxed vibrations.

Real meaning is present, impression by impression. Attention flows to meet each impression before mentation labels and categorizes it. Ordinarily I miss the meaning, because the attention is occupied with the coarse, dead level of reactions to impressions.

The Still Small Voice

The Book of Kings I features two mighty prophets, Elijah and Elisha. Both performed miracles. Elisha performed twice as many miracles as Elijah, yet Elijah has always been considered the mightier of the two. Why?

Elijah's secret seems to be the monumental discovery, made in a quiet moment that was the culmination of a stormy career, that the path to healing social evils is an inward one.

Appalled by the injustice he saw all around him, Elijah confronted king, priests and the multitudes with their stupidity and evil deeds. His challenge led to a dramatic showdown between the power of God and the powers of the idols. The power of God, manifested through Elijah, prevailed, yet Elijah himself was defeated. Withdrawing to the desert, in exasperation and despair, he had a vision. The authentic presence of God appears neither in wind, nor in earthquake or fire, but in a still small voice.

Unlike Zen teachings, the Old Testament does not abound in paradoxes. And yet, here it is: the experience of mystery, unveiled as a paradox. How can God's voice be still? And how can stillness be a voice?

The resolution of the paradox seems to lie not in the terms of the paradox, but in the being of the prophet. In extremity beyond despair, he *was* the still small voice. Having *been* it, he heard it. Always, we only hear what we are.

Following that supreme moment, Elijah hears what his task is to be in the field of history. He returns from the desert, anoints two kings, and his successor, the prophet Elisha. And, as the story unfolds, one is left with the impression that in the field of history Elijah's activities were not overwhelmingly successful. Evil people and evil deeds continue to abound— and Elisha as well had an uphill battle on his hands. But, somehow, we are not surprised. How could it be otherwise? Human nature being what it is, the drama of history unfolds as a slow, halting ascent.

Viewed from a wide perspective, however, the story of Elijah is an unqualified success. Both the biblical text and popular legends depict him as a man who was not subject to death. This deathlessness is, perhaps, as echo of the indubitable, miraculous fact, that, whatever happens to the prophet, the experience of the still small voice is very much alive.

They Are All Angels

"They are all angels," said Bill [Segal]
He was contemplating the dense crowd of depressed,
distracted bodies crammed together in the Paris metro.
"They are all angels," he repeated. "But they don't know it!"
                                                    —Peter Brook

It is a lovely Saturday morning. Farmers market at the village green. People move without haste, children are running around, friends meet and chat . . .

I sit on a bench, look and enjoy. And yet...there is a tugging at the heart. Does the appearance reveal the truth? Is this village green, at this time and place, really a piece of paradise, a haven in this insane world?

In a way, it is. An invisible rain of ease and calm has descended, and knowingly or not, we are all affected. But if one is to bask in it, is it better not to look too closely?

As if to illustrate this, an elderly colleague of mine appears down the path. The poor man had a stroke—now he is dragging his leg, and his face is contorted. I saw him a few weeks ago, and he looks better this morning. "Better," however, is a relative term. The man is a fighter. He battles his condition in a state of grim determination. His determination is fueled by pure rage. Now he is somewhat more relaxed, but the understructure of rage shows through.

People are kind to each other this morning, within their limitations. The good-hearted lady who sells corn can only express her goodwill through a painted smile. And today with her good heart flowing over, her smile is even more painted—as if the real feelings, unable to push through the mask, strain it. In another sense they have pushed through, as they always do. The mask is a net. Her grandchildren love her.

Our rigidity is softened this morning both from above and from below, as if the inner and the outer strive to meet in us. Their struggle is our pain and our joy. At any rate, the little kid in front of me has no problem. All he wants is to splash in the round fountain, and all his mother wants is to prevent him from doing so. My heart goes to the child, but he is bound to lose. It is a big, black dog that comes next, jumps in the fountain, enjoys and elicits a general smile.

A beautiful drama is being enacted here this morning, on a sunny stage. The characters are true, playing their parts to perfection, down to the smallest detail. For a brief moment one could almost believe that they know it—but this is merely the illusion of the writer, playing his own part.

> ... We had the experience but missed the meaning.
> And approach to the meaning restores the experience
> In a different form, beyond any meaning
> We can assign to happiness.
>
> —T. S. Eliot, *The Four Quartets*

The Presence of God

I wish for the presence of God, while another "I," the usual one, has no such wish—and has, moreover, a concept of God that has nothing to do with God.

The experience shows that a part of me, a part that is reachable, needs no mental understanding of the concept of God, and in fact, has a relationship, or at least a wish for a relationship, with the ineffable that the word *God* indicates. This is a remarkable discovery.

This discovery cannot be translated into a program of action. I feel the need to tread lightly here. Who is the one who is writing now, and what does he want? This question stopped me in my tracks. There is a certain atmosphere, one of relaxation and ease, that characterizes the one who remembers God. My usual self has a deep feeling of dissatisfaction at its core. The longing that the other Self feels is of a different quality. There is no hurry in it, no desperate groping after reflections as if they were the substance. There is clean honesty in the feeling of longing, in the willingness to actively wait, in having the feelings alive in the moment, in feeling the foretaste of fulfillment in the very longing.

Remembering myself now brings with it the freedom to allow a change from the constricted self to the other: an inner shift. Everything begins with this inner shift. This much stands to reason—for how could a constricted self receive the presence of God?

In the inner shift—I feel it now—there is an opening to the impersonal side and a letting go of the personal. I am in touch with myself as a vehicle of pure awareness. I look at my awareness, and it is just awareness.

Now the following comes to me: It is possible to be in the service of the Divine before having the clear experience of it, precisely by practicing this inner shift. At this moment the feeling of longing is palpable. Allowing it to be, being impersonal, open, trying to be in tune with a subtle and indefinable vibration—is such a service.

The Power of a Kiss

Personal preferences cast away.
Attention is open to an unknown, vast world.
The attention was attached to things and states,
Now it is attracted toward the unknown,
Toward being absorbed.
Open to be changed through delving, through participation,
Attention is the food of Self,
Fulfilled by being eaten.
Ordinary attention transformed into extraordinary energy,
Self acquires a channel to work in the world.
Working in the world, Self transforms it.
At every turn, frogs turn into princes, through the power of a kiss.

A drop
Rolling down my sleeve—
Eternity.